Do Animals Have Rights?

ISSUES FOR THE NINETIES

Volume 3

Editor

Craig Donnellan

Independence

Educational Publishers

First published by Independence
PO Box 295
Cambridge CB1 3XP

British Library Cataloguing in Publication Data
Do Animals Have Rights? – (Issues for the Nineties Series)
I. Donnellan, Craig II. Series
179.3

ISBN 1 872995 50 0

Printed in Great Britain
at Haynes Cannon
Wellingborough
Northamptonshire

Cover
The cartoon on the front cover is by
the artist, Ken Pyne.

CONTENTS

Introduction

Do Animals Have Rights? is the third volume in the series:
Issues For The Nineties. The aim of this series is to offer
up-to-date information about important issues in our
world.

Do Animals Have Rights? examines the use of animals in
medical experiments and the debate about animal sports.
The information comes from a wide variety of sources and
includes:

Government reports and statistics
Newspaper reports, features
Magazine articles and surveys
Literature from lobby groups
and charitable organisations.

It is hoped that, as you read about the many aspects of the
issues explored in this book, you will critically evaluate
the information presented. It is important that you decide
whether you are being presented with facts or opinions.
Does the writer give a biased or an unbiased report? If an
opinion is being expressed, do you agree with the writer?

Do Animals Have Rights? offers a useful starting point for
those who need convenient access to information about
the many issues involved. However, it is only a starting
point. At the back of the book is a list of organisations
which you may want to contact for further information.

One of the first people you should consult is your librarian.
He or she is an important resource person who can offer
you valuable assistance in your search for additional
information.

*****

Medical research and animal rights

From the Research for Health Charities Group

The ethics

• From earliest times, people and animals have lived together. The way we live with animals in our society causes strong feelings, and is often discussed in newspapers, on TV and the radio.

• Some people say that all animals (including tiny insects such as fleas) have equal rights to humans, and we should not do anything to an animal which we would not also do to another person.

• Most people agree that we have a duty to treat animals as well as we can, but that people should come first. The law protects both humans and animals from bad treatment.

• Society says that it is alright to use animals in many ways such as for food, clothing, shelter, entertainment, education and to help us work. There are many animal products in daily use in most homes.

• Sometimes animals are killed because of the damage that they do to our crops, or our homes and possessions. Animals are killed because we think they are dangerous, or, because they can spread diseases. Some animals are killed just because people do not like them.

• We recognise that some animals have a special relationship with humans, such as cats and dogs, or are very like us such as apes and monkeys. Society has passed laws to give these animals extra protection.

• There are often conflicting interests, for instance when animals are studied in veterinary research so that many other animals can benefit.

• Both people and animals are also studied for human medicine to help us understand diseases. They can help us in studies where a living system is needed; where effects on more than one organ or system (such as the blood circulation) need to be studied; and in learning how diseases and other characteristics are passed on from one generation to the next.

• After a disease has been identified, and a possible treatment found, animals are once more used to show whether it is safe enough to try the treatment in humans. Different animal species may have different responses, which can give us valuable information about the way some people may react.

• For example guinea pigs can be made ill by very large doses of the medicine penicillin because it kills the bacteria which live in their guts, which in turn poisons the guinea pig. Even though it saves thousands of lives every year, many people are made ill by penicillin, for exactly the same reason as the guinea pigs.

• After a disease has been understood, and after a treatment has been found, a pharmaceutical company may then be able to make a medicine.

• All medicines are dangerous, and toxicity tests (poison tests) have to be done on laboratory tissues and some animals before they are done on humans. After testing on people the medicine can go into normal use, although some people may still be allergic to it. Household, garden and industrial products are all tested in the same way.

The above was reproduced from a student information pack published by the Research for Health Charities Group. See page 39 for details.

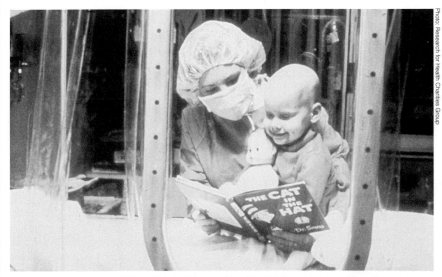

Photo: Research for Health Charities Group

The development of many major medical treatments has also depended on animal research.

Opposing views about medical research and animal rights

Statements by animals rights groups and animal welfare charities.

● 'The majority of animals used in experiments are not given anaesthetic'.

BUAV Christmas catalogue 1993

● 'Home Office statistics show that in Great Britain some 80% of animal experiments are conducted without anaesthetic at any stage . . . Vivisectors defend such experiments by saying they are no worse that minor injections or blood sampling, 'just a pinprick', such as might be experienced by any patient in a doctor's surgery. They are lying. As standard experimental techniques show with blood sampling, the simplest way to obtain blood from a rat is to chop off its head. This can be done by first stunning the rat with a blow to the back of the head and then cutting partially or completely through the neck with strong scissors. Since this is the simplest method, it is probably the one most commonly used'.

NAVS leaflet 'Just a Pinprick' distributed 1992.

● 'Lots of experiments are conducted on animals for no reason whatsoever, and for reasons that have got nothing to do with the health and safety of human beings'.

BUAV, Fox FM Radio 09.02.93.

● 'Through our Health With Humanity campaign we have pointed out the simple truth that animal experiments tell us about animals and not people. This is the view that is shared by 88 per cent of British doctors'.

BUAV, Harlow Star 21.01.93.

● '. . . the evidence shows quite clearly that animal experiments are of no value whatsoever to doctors'.

*Dr. Vernon Coleman, Plan 2000
South Shields Gazette 12.10.93.*

● 'Animal experiments have resulted in wide ranging benefits to humans and other animals. This is not a matter of opinion but is a simple fact which can be demonstrated. Sadly some vociferous animal activists state that animal experiments have never assisted anyone. Unfortunately such prejudice does the cause of animal welfare serious harm and alienates many people who could be of great assistance in the search for alternatives'.

*'Animal Experiments and Their Alternatives',
Merlin Books 1987 (publication funded by the
Dr. Hadwen Trust for Humane Research)*

Statements by the government, doctors, medical research charities and scientists

● 'Most procedures are so minor that the use of anaes-thesia is not appropriate. One third (33%) of procedures started in 1992 either used anaesthesia with recovery or were procedures in which the only anaesthesia was terminal'.

*HMSO Statistics of Scientific Procedures
on Living Animals 1992.*

● 'The strict legal controls on animal research, in the Animals (Scientific Procedures) Act 1986, do not allow animals to be used to obtain information that is obtainable by other means. Funds for biomedical research are limited, so each research proposal is rigorously assessed by panels of experts. Trivial, irrelevant or repetitive work will not attract funding'.

BRET leaflet 'Myth Versus Reality' 1992.

● 'In determining whether and on what terms to grant a project license the Secretary of State shall weigh the likely adverse effects on animals concerned against the benefit likely to accrue as a result of the programme to be specified in the license'.

Animals (Scientific Procedures) Act 1986.

● 'The Secretary of State shall not grant a project license authorising the use of cats, dogs, primates or equidae (horses) unless he is satisfied that animals of no other species are suitable for the purposes of the programme to be specified in the license or that it is not practicable to obtain animals of any other species that are suitable for those purposes'.

Animals (Scientific Procedures) Act 1986.

● 'Almost 85 per cent of a sample of doctors surveyed by the BMA support animal experimentation. This was the number who believed that a ban on such experiments would affect medical development'.

BMA, Lancashire Evening Post 08.08.93.

● 'That the BMA undertake a publicity campaign to inform the public about the past, present and future importance of human and animal experimentation in the fight against disease and illness, and in the maintenance of good health in both humans and other animal species'.

BMA Conference resolution July 1992.

*The above was reproduced from a student information pack published by
the Research for Health Charities Group. See page 39 for details.
September, 1994*

The moral issue

From Animal Aid

As members of human society we live by moral codes designed to protect our weaker members. We take care of the sick, old and disabled and punish those who are violent towards others.

These qualities of compassion and justice are part of being human. But we also have a darker side. A selfish, cruel side which is responsible for violence and destruction.

It is to these aspects of human nature which vivisection appeals. We experiment on animals because they are powerless to stop us and we count their pain as unimportant when measured against our own interests. We live unhealthy lives and make animals suffer in the search for cures for our ills. We even see the production of a new lipstick or oven cleaner as a good enough reason to inflict pain on animals.

It's not that we think animals can't feel pain – we know very well that they do. And it is dangerous to say that we use animals in experiments because they lack our intelligence. After all, this argument would also allow us to experiment on mentally handicapped humans.

We use animals because we have decided that our species is so important that other species should suffer for our benefit.

In recent history we've seen a chilling extension of this way of thinking. In the concentration camps of Nazi Germany and Japan, during the Second World War, scientists experimented on human prisoners alongside animals – for the sake of the 'master race'.

Even today scientists are beginning to experiment on aborted, but still living, human foetuses.

Animals have feelings. Like us, they can suffer pain, fear and mental agony. Like us, each has a life to live. A rat's life is important to a rat whatever value a human may place on it! Why should one individual animal be made to suffer for the supposed benefit of people (or other animals)? Would it be right to kill one human being in an experiment if it would save thousands of others? What if that human were you?

As important as it is, the case against vivisection does not rely on the mass of evidence which shows that it is bad science. It rests on the belief that it is morally wrong to deliberately harm those weaker than ourselves – whether they belong to our own, or to another species.

© Animal Aid
September, 1994

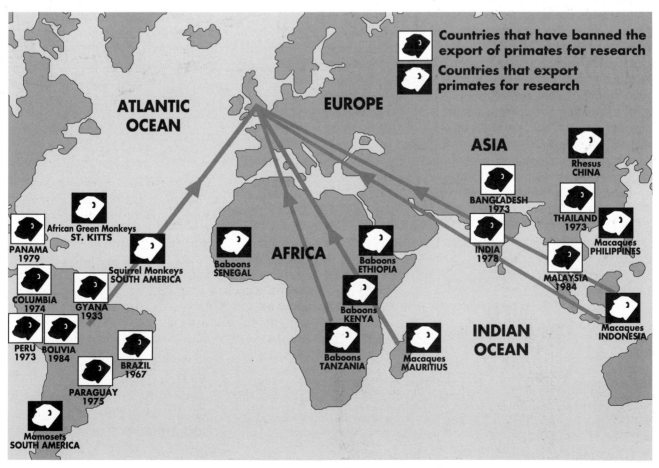

Animals in scientific research

The statistics

Background information

The use of animals in experiments in the UK is controlled by law – the *Animals (Scientific Procedures) Act 1986*. This law applies to: 'any experimental or other scientific procedure applied to an animal which may have the effect of causing that animal pain, suffering, distress or lasting harm'.

The act only covers vertebrate animals except for octopus which was included in 1993.

A scientific procedure is anything done to an animal relating to scientific research or testing. The procedure may be experimental (such as giving an animal a drug to see if it heals ulcers) or non-experimental (such as taking blood from an animal to make use of something in the blood).

The act is administered by the Home Office and its team of inspectors. Under the act three licences are needed before animals can be used. These are:

- The Certificate of Designation for the place where the work is carried out. (*Places where animals are bred for research must also have this certificate*).
- The Project Licence for the programme of research.
- The Personal Licence for the person carrying out the work.

Before a project licence is granted, any adverse effects on the animal must be weighed against the proposed benefits of the research.

Each year the Home Office collects information about the projects and procedures started during that year. This information is provided by the project licence holder and includes details of:

- The numbers of animals used.
- The species of animals used.
- The procedures involved.
- The purpose of the work.

Uses of animals in research and testing, 1992 Total procedures: 2,928,258			
Purpose	**Number**	**Approximate % of total**	
Development of medical/dental products and appliances			
Toxicity tests	284,397	(9.7)	
Non-toxicity tests	904,819	(30.9)	**40.6%**
Development of veterinary products and appliances			
Toxicity tests	29,644	(1.0)	
Non-toxicity tests	124,979	(4.3)	**5.3%**
Fundamental studies of body structure and function	627,383		**21.4%**
Production/maintenance of sera, tumours and infectious agents	416,127		**14.2%**
Safety evaluation			
Industrial products	91,832	(3.1)	
Agricultural products	76,986	(2.6)	
Environmental pollution	59,192	(2.0)	
Food additives	6,134	(0.2)	
Household products	2,080	(0.1)	
Cosmetics	2,164	(0.1)	
Other	20,214	(0.7)	**8.8%**
Breeding for genetic defects	177,996		**6.1%**
Miscellaneous uses, diagnosis, surgical techniques, education/training	104,311		**3.6%**

The Home Office uses this information to produce a booklet called *Statistics of Scientific Procedures on Living Animals, Great Britain*. Details of procedures carried out one year are published the next year. For example, the statistics for 1993 were published in July 1994.

More detailed information can be found in the RSPCA publication: *A Guide to the Home Office Booklet 'Statistics of Scientific Procedures on Living Animals', Great Britain*.

The statistics

The number of scientific procedures on animals started during 1992 was 2,928,258. The actual number of animals used was slightly lower, at 2,854,046. This is because some animals are used more than once in certain controlled circumstances. The purposes of the procedures are shown in the table above.

© The Royal Society for the Prevention of Cruelty to Animals (RSPCA) September, 1994

What medical advances have come from animal research?

From the Biomedical Research Education Trust

Medical research in the last 100 years has produced many ways to treat and prevent diseases. Table 1 lists some of the main discoveries in basic research which relied on animal experiments. The development of many major medical treatments has also depended on animal research. Table 2 lists some better known examples of these. Without research on animals, few if any of these would have been discovered.

Table 1
Major advances in basic research that depended on animal experiments

1600s
Discovery of blood circulation
Discovery of the function of the lungs

1700s
Measurement of blood pressure

1800s
Vaccination to stimulate immunity
Understanding of infectious diseases

1900s
Discovery of antibodies
Understanding of hormone systems

1920s
Discovery of vitamins

1930s
Discovery of the mechanism of nerve impulses
Discovery of tumour viruses

1940s
Understanding of embryonic development

1950s
Understanding of the control of muscle activity
Understanding of energy metabolism
Understanding the mechanism of hearing

1960s
Discovery of monoclonal antibodies
Understanding the biochemical functions of the liver

1970s
Understanding of transplantation antigens
Understanding the way the brain functions
Discovery of prostaglandins

1980s
Development of transgenic animals
Understanding the basis of memory

Table 2
Major medical advances that depended on animal research

1920s
Insulin for diabetes

1930s
Modern anaesthetics for surgery
Diphtheria vaccine

1940s
Broad-spectrum antibiotics for infections
Whooping cough vaccine
Heart-lung machine for open-heart surgery

1950s
Kidney transplants
Cardiac pacemakers and replacement heart valves
Polio vaccine
Drugs for high blood pressure
Hip replacement surgery

1960s
Rubella vaccine
Coronary bypass operations
Heart transplants
Drugs to treat mental illness
Corneal transplants

1970s
Drugs to treat ulcers
Improved sutures and other surgical techniques
Drugs to treat asthma
Drugs to treat leukaemia

1980s
Immunosuppressant drugs for organ transplants
CAT scanning for improved diagnosis
Life-support systems for premature babies
Drugs to treat viral disease.

© *Biomedical Research Education Trust*
December, 1994

Animal experiments

Ever since animal experiments (or vivisection) began, people have protested against them.

In 1876 the first Act governing animal experiments was passed but it did nothing to control the spread of vivisection. Now, over a century later, millions more animals die in experiments.

What law governs vivisection?

It is called the Animals (Scientific Procedures) Act 1986. It allows even the most trivial experiments and increases the secrecy surrounding vivisection. People working in laboratories will now be breaking the law if they reveal confidential information about what goes on to the public.

Which species of animals are used in experiments?

Mice, rats, guinea pigs, rabbits, cats, dogs, monkeys, birds, reptiles and fish are the species most commonly used. Horses and farm animals are also sometimes experimented upon and a new breed of 'mini pig' has been bred specially for the laboratory. Researchers hope the public will not have as much sympathy for pigs as for animals like cats and dogs.

Where do laboratories get animals from?

Laboratory animal breeding centres provide animals for use in experiments. Some suppliers will even breed animal 'freaks' like hairless mice.

Most laboratory monkeys once lived in the wild. They are trapped and sent to laboratories all over the world. Many die during capture and transportation.

How is information about vivisection obtained?

Reports of experiments are published in scientific magazines and journals. The Government also publishes yearly figures on the number and species of animals used and the types of experiments performed. As it is virtually impossible to obtain photographs of British experiments, most of the photographs come from abroad. These are used to illustrate the same sorts of experiments performed in this country.

Are the experiments painful?

Is it painful to be electric shocked, burned, maimed and poisoned?

These are just some of the 'procedures' carried out on laboratory animals who, like us, have an advanced nervous system.

Legally, researchers apply for a licence to inflict 'mild', 'moderate' or 'substantial' pain and suffering on animals and the vast majority of all the animals used in experiments are not given anaesthetic. Even when anaesthetics are given, this is often only for the first part of the experiment, during surgical operations on the animal's brain or body.

Animals also suffer mentally from life in a laboratory where they are imprisoned in small cages. Highly sensitive, sociable species like monkeys can be literally driven mad by long periods of solitary confinement in barren cages.

Why are animal experiments allowed to continue?

So far British governments have refused to ban even experiments to test yet more unnecessary cosmetics. Unfortunately vivisection has become a scientific 'tradition'. It is now a huge and powerful industry that provides profit for a network of breeders, suppliers and cage and equipment manufacturers, as well as those scientists and technicians who make a career out of vivisection.

Is 'Advocates' opposed to all animal experiments?

Yes, we want to see an end to all animal experiments. There is much evidence to show that vivisection is unjustified on scientific grounds as it is misleading and unproductive as a source of information on human disease. In 1991, approximately 32 million animals were used in experiments
© Animal Aid, November, 1994

Medical research and drug testing

From Animal Aid

Each year over one million animals have their bodies and brains damaged, are given painful diseases or implanted with cancerous tumours in medical research.

Much of this research is repetitive or pointless, yielding results which do not apply to humans.

Also thousands of unnecessary drugs with similar ingredients, but different brand names, are produced just for profit. These are known as 'me-too' drugs. How many different headache pills, pain killers and other drugs do we need?

The World Health Organisation estimates that only 200 drugs (approximately) are necessary to human health . . . yet there are an incredible 18,000 medicaments containing 3,000 active components on the British market alone.

We all want to find ways of preventing ill health and treating diseases like cancer, heart disease and AIDS. But laboratory animals have not provided and will not provide the answers we are looking for.

Kill or cure?

Animal experiments are unreliable because different species react to substances in different ways – so results of animal tests cannot be applied to humans with any certainty. For example:

Penicillin is a useful drug for humans but it kills guinea pigs and hamsters.

Morphine sedates humans but causes frenzied behaviour in cats.

Chloroform, an anaesthetic for humans, kills dogs.

Aspirin causes birth deformities in many species including rats, cats and dogs – but not in humans.

Digitalis, a useful heart drug for humans, causes dangerously high blood pressure in dogs.

Photo: Animal Aid

Animal experiments are unreliable because different species react to substances in different ways.

All drugs are tested on animals but there is no way of knowing what the result will be in humans. Ciba Geigy, a major drug company, estimated that 95% of drugs passed as safe in animal tests are rejected at the next stage . . . clinical trials on people.

In the past some drugs have been withdrawn after causing severe side effects and in some cases killing patients. These drugs include *Flenac, Osmosin, Flosint, Eraldin* and the arthritis drug *Opren* which harmed thousands of patients and caused 60 deaths in Britain alone.

Many other drugs cause more subtle damage and some like the tranquillisers Valium and Librium are dangerously addictive.

Animal experiments not only fail to warn of the danger of some drugs but can hamper the development of useful medicines when tests on animals reveal side effects which would not occur in people.

Cancer research

Countless millions of animals have died in cancer research but very little progress has been made in dealing with most human cancers. The World Health Organisation estimates that over 80% of cancers are preventable. Cancer is mainly caused by factors like smoking, bad diet and exposure to cancer-causing substances like some industrial chemicals. Chemicals suspected of causing cancer can legally pollute our air, water and food (food additives).

Until we concentrate on reducing and eliminating the causes of cancer the terrible death toll will continue.

© Animal Aid
November, 1994

Why is animal research necessary?

From the Biomedical Research Education Trust

Because the whole living body is so complicated simple laboratory models are nowhere near good enough. Without animal research we would not have made many important discoveries in medicine. If we stop using animals it is difficult to see how future medical treatments and cures could be achieved.

Over the last 50 years or so our ability to prevent illness and treat sick people has improved greatly. In the 1940s doctors often saw people with diseases like polio that are now very rare in Britain. The number of effective medicines, preventive measures and other treatments that can be prescribed for patients has risen greatly. As a result, more people live to healthy old age and have a better quality of life.

Human biology is very like that of many other animals. This is why results from animal experiments apply to people. Most laboratory animals have the same set of organs: heart, lungs, liver and so on, which work in the same way as they do in people.

Even though there are obvious physical differences, a rat is more like a person than it is different. For example the heart of a rat works in the same way as the human heart. In rats and humans the heart muscle gets oxygen from the blood that flows through the coronary artery. If the flow of blood through a rat's coronary artery decreases, which is what happens in the human heart when people have a heart attack, the same biological changes occur. This can result in sudden death in both species. So medical researchers can use rats to study what happens during heart attacks. Armed with this knowledge, doctors can develop new treatments for human heart patients. Other illnesses can also be researched in animals, and the results from these studies applied to people.

Basic research and medical benefits

Progress in medicine depends on how well we understand basic biology. Knowing how complicated systems work in healthy animals is normally the first step in finding out what happens when something goes wrong. This understanding of the basic biology guides the scientists who develop improved treatments for diseases. Animal research, test-tube experiments, and studies of populations, are all essential steps in basic biological and medical research.

Doing basic research is a bit like digging the foundations of a house. You can't see them, but if they are not there the house will fall down. Science nearly always works in this way, it is not unique to medical research. If early scientists had not studied how electricity was gener-

ated, and how it behaved, it would have been impossible to invent equipment like computers and TVs.

Veterinary medicine

Animal research is just as important in the development of medicines to treat animals. Many of the illnesses suffered by people and animals are the same: examples are cancer, flu, rabies, malaria and many others. Over one third of veterinary medicines are the same as those used in people. We can often use the same medicines in both humans and animals when they suffer from the same illnesses. Heart failure and diabetes are good examples. Heart failure can be treated with digitalis in people and in dogs and horses; diabetes is often treated with insulin injections in humans, cats and dogs. Vets and surgeons may use the same anaesthetics on human or animal patients before surgery, and the same antibiotics to prevent or treat infection. Many techniques of modern surgery were also developed in animals and the same type of surgical operation can be used for both humans and animals.

There are also diseases like distemper which do not affect people but that do affect animals. Distemper affects dogs, seals and dolphins. We can now prevent distemper in dogs in Britain because there is a good vaccine. This vaccine, developed through research using dogs, is given to most dogs when they are puppies.

This raises an interesting question for people who think we should not use animals for research. Would it be right to use animals if you were trying to find cures for other sick animals? If so, why would it be wrong to do the same experiments to find cures for sick people?

Future medical progress

Even today, there are still many diseases that cannot be cured and many existing treatments that could be improved. Just as doctors have a duty to treat patients, medical researchers have a duty to do all they can to help the millions of patients who suffer or die from illnesses like multiple sclerosis, AIDS, muscular dystrophy, cystic fibrosis and Alzheimer's disease. At present we do not have good treatments for these conditions. We should not forget tropical diseases of the developing world – infections like river blindness and liver flukes. Tropical diseases affect about 1800 million people worldwide every year.

With continuing medical research, there is every reason to expect substantial progress during the next 50 years. The use of laboratory animals is vital, because animals are the best available biological models for humans. If animal experiments were banned, the chance of progress in the treatment of disease would be greatly reduced.

Animal research and alternative methods

Some animal rights supporters believe that the results of animal research are not applicable to humans. Doctors and medical scientists throughout the world have shown many times that this belief is wrong and that animal research is important for medical progress. The animal rights organisations also claim that better progress would be made by using 'alternative' test-tube methods and sophisticated computer programs to predict the likely effects of new medicines in humans. The word 'alternative' is misleading when used like this. These techniques are not replacements for animal methods, they have to work alongside them. Test-tube methods and computer programs are an important part of medical research but they give a different type of information from studies on whole animals.

Animals are expensive compared to test-tube methods, so researchers always prefer not to use animals. In fact about 95p out of every £1 spent on medical research in Britain goes on non-animal methods.

Some benefits of animal experimentation

- Discovery of vitamins and understanding of their significance in diet.
- Control of bacterial infections by antibiotics and viral infections by vaccination, e.g. polio, smallpox and measles.
- Determination of blood groups and development of blood transfusion.
- Modern anaesthetics and improved surgical techniques.
- Control of high blood pressure with the reduction in kidney disease and strokes.
- Treatment of neurological disorders, e.g. Parkinson's disease, epilepsy, and of mental illness, e.g. schizophrenia, depression.
- Vaccines and medicines for distemper and hepatitis in dogs, influenza, enteritis and leukaemia in cats, and for many other animal diseases including rabies and anthrax.
- Treatment of childhood leukaemia with chemotherapy, radiotherapy and bone marrow grafts.
- Control of fertility with the contraceptive pill.
- Hip and other joint replacements.
- Development of the heart-lung machine and open heart surgery.
- Renal dialysis for patients with kidney failure.
- Organ transplantation and drugs to fight rejection.
- Corneal transplants and other treatments for serious eye conditions.
- Intensive care techniques for premature babies.

Such test-tube methods alone could not develop new surgical procedures or techniques for intensive care. Without research on animals, surgery would not be the refined science that it is today. Non-animal methods can only play a part in developing a new medicine for epilepsy or high blood-pressure. Cells in a test-tube obviously do not show the symptoms of these diseases. It is difficult to see how non-animal methods by themselves could lead to better treatments for Alzheimer's disease, heart failure or AIDS. New non-animal methods are presently being developed by medical scientists which may reduce the need for animal experiments in future. Everyone would wish that there were real alternatives so that we did not need to use animals; we are still likely to need to do so for the foreseeable future.

Medicines must be effective and safe

The body is much more than just a collection of cells and tissues. The systems that control the different functions of cells and organs are amazingly complex, very sensitive in their control, and specific in their effects. The only alternative to using humans to look at the complex effects of new treatments is the careful and responsible use of laboratory animals. This gives us a lot of information about the effects of these treatments and any possible side-effects. It would be much too dangerous to try out these new chemicals on people. Only if the new medicine passes the animal testing stage will it be tested, under strict medical supervision, on the first human volunteers. In this way we can be reasonably sure that a new treatment is likely to be safe and effective.

In practice, animal research, test-tube methods, computer technology, and human studies, are used together to tackle difficult medical problems. Medical advances for both people and animals will depend on medical research that includes some careful, humane use of animals.

© Biomedical Research Education Trust December, 1994

Why do we use animals for research?

From the Humane Research Trust

Is it because:

- They are less intelligent than us?
- They feel pain less than us?
- Their lives are not as important as ours?
- They are weaker than us?
- We have traditionally used them and it has become acceptable?
- There is no other way for progress?

Let us consider each question in turn

We use animals because they are less intelligent than us.

Most animals are classed as less 'intelligent' than humans, but what exactly is meant by this expression? By 'less intelligent' do we mean they cannot speak, or that they cannot stand up for themselves, or even think?

True, animals cannot speak, and neither can they defend themselves against man, but this does not mean they cannot think. Neither does any of this diminish their ability to suffer pain and distress. If we are going to classify creatures by how intelligent *we* think they are, then this is a form of discrimination that could easily be applied to humans – and no one would accept that.

They feel less pain than we do.

We can never know how much pain another person feels, we can only imagine it because we know what it feels like to be in pain ourselves. Similarly, we can never know how much pain an animal feels, but we can imagine it. Most higher animals have a nervous system similar to our own. If we consider the prerequisites for pain are a central nervous system connected to pain receptors, there is no reason at all to suppose animals feel any less pain than we do. Indeed on the basis of this, most scientists use animals for pain research *because* their pain is like ours. Besides, animals show when they are in pain – if you kick a dog it will yelp; if you insert tubes into the brains of conscious rats they will feel pain.

We use animals because their lives are not as important as ours.

Feelings on this subject may very much depend on religious views, or feelings about life in general. For those who see humans as the centre of the universe with everything at *their* disposal for *their* convenience, then animals will merely be there to eat, wear, and use at their will. This attitude is called 'speciesism'.

On the other hand, it can be argued that all life is equally valuable and should be treated with respect. It must be remembered though, experiments are carried out on live animals and the level of suffering must be taken into account as well as the importance of life itself.

We use animals in research because they are weaker than us.

If we cause suffering to animals in laboratories because they are weaker than we are, we are acting in a disgraceful way – like bullies attacking someone smaller than themselves. There have been times in the past when people were experimented on because they were powerless and the perpetrators of this were eventually punished. So how is what we are doing to animals any different?

We use animals because we have traditionally used them.

Things that have always been are often taken for granted, but this does not necessarily mean they are right. The slave trade, inhumane as it was, was acceptable to many people because things had always been that way. Progress and changes for the better only happen when people start thinking differently.

Indeed looking back, scientific evidence seems to suggest that animal testing has hindered the progress of medical research.

We use animals because there is no other way.

There are other ways – *and better ones too*. The Humane Research Trust believes that non-animal medical research is not only more humane, but more reliable too. After all, what would you prefer – taking medicine that has been tested on a mouse, or taking medicine that has been tested on human cells just like your own?

The moral issues

Today we accept that all humans should have equal rights whatever their colour or sex. We use words like 'racism' or 'sexism' to describe attitudes that are unfair to certain groups. We believe that how we treat people should not depend on the country of their birth, nor whether they are a man or woman, but on the fact that they are all people and deserve to be treated with equal consideration.

We say all this because people have rights. This means it is important to each person what happens to them. We do not want to be hungry or cold, frightened or hurt because these things cause us to suffer. Animals also have rights. They do not choose to suffer either and they too should be treated with equal consideration. A lack of concern for other creatures simply because they are of a different species is called 'speciesism'.

Animals do not need the same rights as us. A puppy does not need to vote and a cat does not need the right to a good education, but all animals are entitled to the right not to suffer. Scientists accept that animals feel pain just the way we do, so do we have the right to make animals suffer? Man is an animal too – just a different species.

The Rev Andrew Linzey in his book *Christianity and the Rights of Animals* condemns all experiments – whether on animals, criminals or embryos. He believes people justify them on the basis of benefit – the benefit of one creature at the expense of another. This philosophy inevitably justifies other evils and if our thinking is dominated by this utilitarian attitude, then there is 'no right, value or good which cannot be bargained away'.

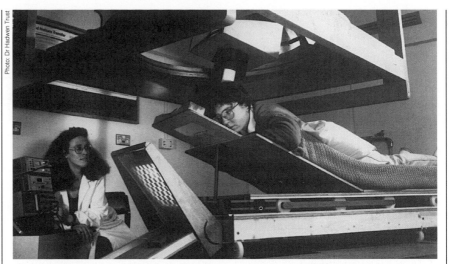

The Dr Hadwen Trust is funding vision research with MEG, a new scanner which could replace brain experiments on animals.

'I believe if you can find it in your heart and mind to empathise with and respect non human life, then I think your capacity, your capability, for love is that much greater. Joining this movement is like "loving thy neighbour" in its highest sense.'

Donald Barnes – American National Anti-Vivisection Society

Medical and non medical experiments

Many people feel that animals must suffer if the end result is better for people, but they object to animals being used in laboratories for other reasons. For example, it may be considered wrong to use an animal to test a new lipstick or shampoo, but if it is to try and develop a new drug that may save lives, then that might be considered a good enough reason to use animals. But before you decide, consider the following:

1 Does an animal suffer any more or less whether it is a weedkiller, a cosmetic or a medicine that is being tested?

2 Since there are alternatives that are practical, effective and safer, would it not make sense and be more civilised to use those instead of animals? Those who oppose us (such as scientists who use animals or breeders who sell animals) often accuse us of caring more for animals than people, but this is nonsense.

Those committed to animal welfare are equally committed to human welfare.

3 Many medical experiments carried out on animals are because people damage their own health, either through a bad diet, smoking or drinking too much and not taking proper exercise. Should animals suffer because we allow ourselves to become ill through bad habits?

4 There are already thousands of medicines available in this country for some minor illness such as headaches and coughs, there are already many preparations on the market. Do we really need so many medicines?

5 When a pharmaceutical company brings a new drug on to the market, they can patent it for many years.

This means no other firm is allowed to make and sell that particular drug. The other firms want to make money by selling that kind of drug, so they produce one almost the same but with a slightly different formula. These are called 'me too' drugs. Should medicines be produced just to make a profit for the firms that manufacture them?

Are medicines always the best thing for our health? We all hear stories of being addicted to drugs, terrible side effects, along with many cases of over treatment and bad treatment. Is taking drugs the answer?

The above is an extract from the Humane Research Trust's education pack. See page 39 for address details.

© Humane Research Trust December, 1994

Animal experimentation

From FRAME (Fund for the Replacement of Animals in Medical Experiments)

What are laboratory animals used for?

Animals are used in experiments because of their broad similarity to ourselves. We use animals for some purposes that would not be allowed in humans.

Experiments are carried out on living animals for five main reasons:

1. Improving basic knowledge about the complicated biological systems (e.g. the nervous system) which keep humans and other animals alive and well, and understanding the effects of diseases on these systems.

2. Devising new methods for diagnosing disease (e.g. cancer, heart disease).

3. Developing new treatments for various diseases, including better medicines and surgical techniques.

4. Producing useful biological products which can be used in the prevention and treatment of diseases (e.g. vaccines, insulin for diabetics).

5. Safety (toxicity) testing, to provide information on the potential dangers to humans from chemicals and products, such as medicines, household products (e.g. washing powder), cosmetics and toiletries (e.g. hair-dyes, sunscreens, toothpaste), chemicals used in agriculture (e.g. week-killers) and industry (e.g. acids) and food additives (e.g. colourings).

How many animals are used?

Every year the Government publishes statistics on the scientific procedures carried out on living animals in Great Britain. 3,242,449 procedures were undertaken in 1991. The numbers of experiments have declined steadily since 1970. However, the figures for 1991 were slightly higher than those for 1990.

Most of the procedures carried out on animals in 1991 were con-cerned with developing and testing new medical and veterinary products. Consumer concern has influenced the use of animals in testing cosmetics, toiletries and household products, and the numbers of animals used in these areas have fallen dramatically in Britain. However, a greater aware-ness of the impact of chemicals on our environment (e.g. acid rain, fertilisers) has led to an increasing number of animals being used in certain tests.

What are the benefits?

Many major medical and veterinary advances have depended heavily upon animal research. As a result, human and animal suffering, illness and early death have been reduced. Some examples of medical advances made through animal research are the development of:

- Medicines e.g. antibiotics and analgesics, and medicines for treating asthma and diabetes;
- Vaccines e.g. for polio, measles and whooping cough;
- Surgical techniques e.g. heart surgery and organ transplantation;
- Medical technology e.g. life-support machines for keeping premature babies alive.

What are the costs?

The costs to the animals used in scientific procedures can be substantial. They can involve suffering caused by the conditions under which the animals are held and by the scientific procedures themselves. The total suffering in any project also depends upon how sentient the species is and the number of animals used. So, when deciding the costs to the animals of a particular procedure, several factors must be taken into account. These include the number of animals to be used, how they are going to be killed, and whether anaesthetics or analgesics are going to be used.

How is animal experimentation controlled?

In the UK, the Animals (Scientific Procedures) Act 1986 and Directive 86/609 from the European Economic Community (EEC) place controls upon the use of protected animals in experiments. Non-animal methods must be used whenever possible and animal suffering must be minimised. The 1986 Act requires that the project, the researcher and the premises all have licences. The Act also requires that the Home Secretary, in consultation with a team of experts, weighs the balance between the predicted suffering of the animals protected under the terms of the Act and the potential benefits of a piece of research, before a licence is granted for that project. Home Office inspectors regularly visit laboratories to check that the terms of the Act are upheld.

Which organisations are involved?

Thousands of organisations throughout the world are concerned with the issues of animal experimentation and vivisection. In Britain, there are hundreds of groups, but they can be divided into three main categories.

The anti-vivisectionist

The anti-vivisectionists campaign for an immediate and total end to animal experiments. There are four main anti-vivisection organisations, the National Anti-Vivisection Society (NAVS), the British Union for the Abolition of Vivisection (BUAV), Animal Aid and Advocates for Animals.

'Animal experiments are both unjust and unnecessary and cannot be justified, for any reason.' NAVS

The defence

These groups campaign in support of the continued use of animals in research and testing. The main organisations are the Research Defence Society (RDS), the Animals in Medicines Research Information Centre (AMRIC) and the Research for Health Charities Group (RHCG)

'Without this research, few of the medicines which we now take for granted would exist, and the chances of finding new or improved treatments in the future would be extremely limited.' AMRIC

The middle ground

Other groups work in between these two positions. There are four main organisations, the Fund for the Replacement of Animals in Medical Experiments (FRAME), the British Veterinary Association (BVA), the Universities Federation for Animal Welfare (UFAW) and the Royal Society for the Prevention of Cruelty to Animals (RSPCA). These groups argue that there will be a 'tragic necessity' to carry out some animal experimentation for the foreseeable future, but that greater efforts should be made to find non-animal methods (i.e. alternatives).

'As long as animals continue to be used in experiments, they must be given the maximum protection from pain and suffering, whatever the purpose for which they are used.' RSPCA

FRAME

FRAME was founded in 1969 to promote the concept of alternatives to the use of live animals in medical research and toxicity testing. FRAME believes that the most immediate prospects for real progress lie in reducing the numbers of animals used and refining procedures, so that the suffering of any animals necessarily used is minimised. Our long-term aim of eliminating the need for live animal experiments altogether depends upon the proper development and use of replacement alternative methods. FRAME is actively involved at the forefront of this research.

Strategies for the future

These are three possible ways in which the situation could change:

1. Experiments and tests involving the use of laboratory animals could be banned altogether.

If there was an immediate and total ban on the use of animals, a great deal of basic medical research would be stopped, as would the production of certain vaccines. No new medicines would be developed, and the safety of workers, the general public and patients would be put at risk.

2. Things could continue as now or there could even be an increase in the number of animal experiments. At the present time, we have no effective treatments for many serious diseases, such as heart disease, certain types of cancer, and AIDS. Research using animals may lead to breakthroughs in these areas. However, the 1986 Act and EEC Directive on animal experimentation state that we should be aiming, wherever possible, to reduce the numbers of animals used, and that we should be actively looking for alternatives.

3. There could be a progressive move to reduce, refine and replace the use of animals in experiments.

This is called the Three Rs approach and would appear to be the most sensible way forward. It offers the chance for scientists and animal welfare activists to work together.

In conclusion . . .

The issue of animal experimentation is very complicated. For example, the more animals are like humans, such as monkeys and baboons, the more valuable they are as models for us, but the more we should resist their use as laboratory animals. The use of animal models, because of differences between species, will never provide results which are perfectly relevant to man. However, they do often reveal the unexpected. Non-animal methods tend to tell us expected things and are less likely to reveal the complex interactions which occur in a living animal.

The animal welfare case against animal experimentation is very strong. However, another convincing argument is that it would not be proper to deny the benefits that animal experimentation can offer, both to science and to the sick and suffering, until suitable alternatives for animal procedures have been found.

- FRAME recently published a new series of information sheets. See page 39 for adddress details.

© FRAME)
November, 1994

How many animals are used?

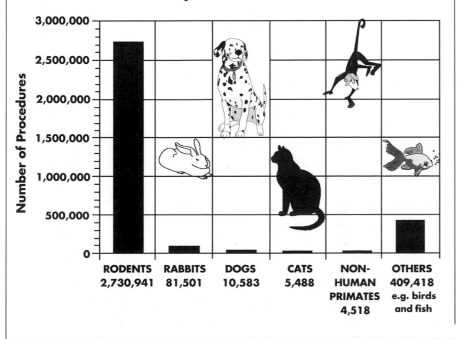

	RODENTS	RABBITS	DOGS	CATS	NON-HUMAN PRIMATES	OTHERS e.g. birds and fish
	2,730,941	81,501	10,583	5,488	4,518	409,418

RSPCA policy on animal experimentation

Pain and suffering in experiments

The RSPCA is opposed to all experiments or procedures which cause pain, suffering or distress.

It is important that, as long as animals continue to be used, every possible effort must be made to prevent suffering. Anaesthesia or other forms of analgesia alone cannot be considered satisfactory solutions to the problem. These are inappropriate, for example, to the problems of fear, hunger and other forms of distress. The whole complex question of the prevention of pain, the relief of suffering and the reduction of distress, must be kept under constant review by those responsible for authorising and carrying out experiments under United Kingdom legislation.

Unnecessary experiments

The RSPCA is opposed to animal experiments which involve unnecessary repetitions, are for scientifically trivial ends, or which involve techniques to which satisfactory and human alternatives have already been developed. The Society is also opposed to the use of animals in the testing of inessential substances, such as cosmetics.

Humane alternatives

The RSPCA supports the development of techniques that will result in the replacement, reduction or refinement of animal experimentation, the concept of the '3 Rs'. The Society regards as an advance any technique which will completely replace the use of animals, reduce the numbers used or reduce suffering.

Examples of *replacement* techniques include cell, tissue and organ cultures; the use of human volunteers in sub-critical studies; the use of epidemiological surveys in human medicine; the use of inanimate models, the use of films and videos in teaching, and more extensive computer analysis. Most replacement techniques are still in their infancy but more could be done to develop them and such work merits Government support.

Techniques leading to *reduction* in the numbers of animals used include the setting up of centralised data banks, adequate prior literature research together with improved experimental design including the use of appropriate statistical methods, the use of films and videos in teaching.

Examples of *refinement* include the use of analgesics; the use of decerebrate animals; the use of purebred animals to reduce numbers needed for statistical analysis; the abolition of death end-points in toxicity and potency tests. The RSPCA believes that refinement offers the best scope for alleviating laboratory animal suffering in the short-term. However, this does not compromise the Society's long-term aim of completely replacing animals in laboratories with alternative techniques.

Legislative and ethical concerns

Animal experimentation in the United Kingdom is controlled by the Animal (Scientific Procedures) Act 1986. Experimentation can only be carried out after licensing by the Home Office and, under the Act, licences should not be granted unless the benefits of the research are considered to outweigh the likely harmful effects on animals. However, the RSPCA believes that the Act can only operate effectively in the interests of animal welfare and as a reflection of public concern if the Government's Animal Procedures Committee uses its extensive powers to investigate project licence applications and reports publicly on these matters.

The RSPCA supports the provisions of the Act that one or more persons be nominated to have overall responsibility for the day-to-day care of the animals in a Scientific Procedure Establishment and that a veterinary surgeon must be appointed to monitor the health and welfare status of these animals but who will be answerable to the Home Secretary.

The importance of appropriate and rigorous training for prospective licensees cannot be overemphasised. The RSPCA believes that the necessary training, not only in the techniques that are to be used and in the recognition and alleviation of pain and suffering, (including analgesia, anaesthesia and euthanasia), but also in the ethical consideration of animal use, should take place before licences are granted.

The RSPCA believes that it is also of vital importance that all new experimental and testing protocols should be subject to extensive ethical review before licences are applied for. The Society encourages the setting up of ethical committees with lay and animal welfare representatives locally in industry, research establishments and universities.

Laboratory animal supply

The RSPCA is opposed to the import and export of laboratory animals. The Society is also strongly opposed to the import of all non-human primates and especially to the use of wild-caught animals of any species. The Society believes that Breeding and Supply Establishments designated under the 1986 Act should be open to inspection by the RSPCA.

© *Royal Society for the Prevention of Cruelty to Animals (RSPCA)*
September, 1994

The hidden price of beauty

From Advocates for Animals

Pain for profit

A growing number of the British public is becoming increasingly concerned and seriously questioning the continued use of animals in research. One area of experimentation which receives universal denunciation is the use of animals in 'cosmetic testing'. The cosmetic business is now often referred to as the 'pain for profit' industry.

The shelves of our shops and stores are already packed to overflowing with cosmetics and toiletries. A number of companies now produce non-animal-tested alternatives. Do we really need more 'pain for profit' products? To help you make up your mind, consider the following standard 'pain for profit' tests.

The draize test

This test is used to study eye irritancy. Rabbits are restrained and the test substance (e.g. shampoo, hairspray, deodorant) is either dripped or sprayed into their eyes. Rabbits are the animal of choice because unlike humans they have no tear ducts as such. So when the substance comes into contact with the eyes, the rabbits are unable to produce tears to wash it away.

A number of tests are carried out over a period of days with each test lasting up to several minutes. The rabbits' eyes are then examined for swelling, damage to the cornea or the conjunctiva. If the test is not halted haemorrhaging, ulceration or blindness can result.

Rabbits suffer excruciating pain in these tests. The pain can be 'slightly' imagined by anyone who has accidentally got shampoo in their eyes.

The draize test is unreliable. In a study of 25 laboratories, researchers

Photo: Animal Aid

Rabbits are restrained and the test substance (e.g. shampoo, hairspray, deodorant) is either dripped or sprayed into their eyes.

admitted that they found extreme variations in test results on rabbits' eyes.

Toxicity or poisoning testing

The test involves forcing varying doses of the test substance (e.g. lipstick ingredients, mouthwash, bubblebath, toothpaste) down the throats of animals (usually rats, mice, guinea-pigs) in order to discover at what dosage half of the animals die.

Almost inevitably this procedure means that all the animals are made seriously ill, some taking two weeks to die, others just managing to survive before they too are killed as the experiment is ended. Common signs of poisoning include unusual vocalisation, restlessness, paralysis, convulsions, irritability, lachrymation (tears), breathlessness, panting, diarrhoea, vomiting, bleeding from the eyes and mouth, tremors, jaundice and of course – death.

This 'crude test' (top toxicologist's own words) is a hit and miss affair. The researcher starts at totally lethal doses and works downwards. It is hard to imagine anyone forcing large amounts of a substance down the throats of struggling and choking animals so that they die. The only guaranteed result is that the amount of suffering caused by this test is considerable.

The skin test

The animals, usually rabbits and guinea-pigs, are restrained and the hair shaved off from an area on their backs. Half of the area is then scraped to expose the sensitive layers of the skin. The substance to be tested (e.g. deodorants, creams, lotions) is then applied. The injury is scored according to its severity after a period of days. Such injury can include bleeding, sores and sometimes the area under test has been eaten away by the substance. Yet more pain and suffering.

Choose cruelty free

Thousands of animals suffered and died in cosmetic testing last year. If you are concerned, this is an area where a boycott of the animal-tested products is not only easy but also very effective – no company likes its name linked with cruelty to animals or lose sales.

We urge you to choose cruelty free products. To help you, we have published a leaflet which lists some of the ranges of non-animal tested alternatives that are available.

See page 39 for address details.

© Advocates for Animals
December, 1994

Animal tests

Many of the leading brands of cosmetics have been tested on animals using these standard tests

Draize eye test

A test substance is dripped into the eyes of rabbits who must suffer the effects over a period of up to seven days. This can eat away at the eye causing swelling, ulceration and even blindness. Normally no pain relief is given.

Skin test

Animals (often rabbits or guinea pigs) have their backs shaved or the hair pulled out with sticky tape. The test substance is applied to their broken skin which can become extremely sore and blistered.

LD50 test

Groups of animals are fed (often by a tube forced down their throats) a test substance to find the dosage which will kill half of them. This dosage is then known as the Lethal Dose 50% (LD50). Reactions can include vomiting, paralysis, convulsions and internal bleeding. Sometimes the animals have to be fed so much of a substance that they die, not from poisoning, but from overloading and damaging the digestive system.

The LD50 test attempts to find out how poisonous a substance is for humans, but many scientists have criticised both this test and the eye and skin tests as being vastly outdated and unreliable.

Most household goods (like disinfectants and cleaners), pesticides, herbicides, food additives, environmental pollutants and industrial chemicals are also developed using these methods.

Psychology experiments

In psychology (or behaviour) experiments animals are given electric shocks, brain damaged, starved, separated from their mothers, deprived of water or made to go without sleep. They are tormented in many different ways and researchers observe their reactions.

'It takes two to make an experiment – the monkey and the man and the best way of judging human behaviour is not by looking at the monkey.'

David Helton, Editor, BBC Wildlife 1984

The number of psychology experiments carried out is growing alarmingly. Researchers claim that animal experiments will help us understand human behaviour and mental illness.

But we can only find out about human behaviour by studying humans! And what we know about mental illness has been gained by observing and counselling mentally ill and disturbed people – not by cruel and inapplicable animal experiments.

Warfare experiments

Animals are irradiated, subjected to poisonous gases, shot, burned and blown up . . . all so that humans can learn more about warfare. In Britain animals are used in warfare experiments at the Porton Down Chemical Defence Establishment in Wiltshire.

© *Advocates for Animal*
September, 1994

Photo: Animal Aid

Rabbits are the animal of choice because, unlike humans, they have no tear ducts as such.

Animal experiments waste time, money and lives

Animal experiments

It must really not be permitted. It is a disgrace to a civilised country.

Queen Victoria

Much medical research aimed at improving *human* health involves experiments on *animals*, and because laboratory animals rarely suffer naturally from human diseases, scientists try to create these conditions artificially.

Monkeys are brain-damaged to study Parkinson's disease; rabbits' joints are chemically inflamed to research rheumatism; cats are infected with lethal viruses; dogs, cats and sheep are damaged with toxins to study respiratory disease; hundreds of thousands of animals are poisoned in toxicity tests for new drugs, food additives and industrial chemicals.

As well as causing pain and suffering, animal experimentation is scientifically unsatisfactory because species variations and the artificiality of animal 'models' can give contradictory and misleading results.

New directions

There are hundreds of paths to scientific knowledge. The cruel ones can teach us only what we ought not to know;

George Bernard Shaw

As the twenty-first century approaches, non-animal techniques are becoming the cutting edge of medical research. Animal experiments are being replaced by a range of alternative methods which frequently prove cheaper, quicker and more effective – as well as saving lives.

● **Computer models** Computer programs can predict the action of medicines and other chemicals with increasing accuracy. At the other end of the size range, whole body systems can also be modelled with computers.

● **Molecular research** Understanding medicine at the molecular level is leading to better treatments for many health problems, including cancer and rheumatism. Individual genes can be pinpointed and manipulated. Virus and bacterial infections can be blocked by tailor-made drugs. Test-tube antibodies are replacing animal tests.

● **Volunteer studies** Volunteer research provides direct information about human health and disease. Cancer, heart disease, muscle disorders, arthritis and psychiatric illness can be researched with new scanners.

Analytical instruments identify and measure tiny doses of test drugs and their fate in the body. Lasers and ultrasound probes can monitor the internal effects of experimental treatments.

● **Population research** Research into the effects of diet, lifestyle and occupation has demonstrated the causes of much heart disease, strokes, cancer, osteoporosis, birth defects and dental decay. Diabetes, arthritis and multiple sclerosis are among major health problems which will be better understood through population research.

● **Test-tube tissues** Human cell cultures are replacing animal tests in medicine research, vaccine production, and in studying and diagnosing infections. Silicon chip sensors and fluorescent dyes are exciting breakthroughs. Cancer, Parkinson's disease, diabetes, glaucoma, spinal injury and multiple sclerosis are also being researched with cell cultures.

● **Micro-organisms** Tests based on bacteria and yeasts can indicate whether a chemical may cause cancer. Luminous bacteria are used to detect products which damage the eye. Yeast-based techniques can predict skin reactions to chemicals.

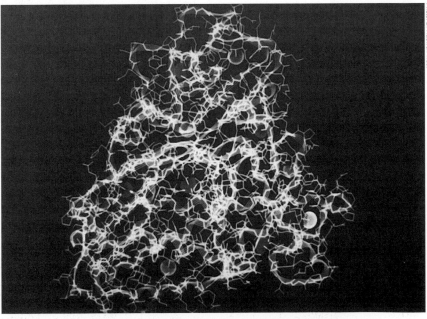

Photo: Dr Hadwen Trust

Computer models allow predictions of toxicity.

Dr Hadwen Trust

The Trust is a medical charity with a special difference: our research benefits people and animals, because our scientists develop and apply *non-animal* techniques, in a wide range of medical fields.

We have more than 21 years' experience of funding top level research programmes which advance medical progress without using animals or animal tissues.

Some of our achievements include:

- Establishing the growth of human cartilage in culture to study *rheumatism*.
- Contributing to the development of Eytex, which measures *eye irritancy* without rabbit tests.
- Developing a new cell culture replaced 200 animals a year in a *diabetes* research laboratory.
- Creating a databank of 4,000 *lymphoma* patients and clinical trials to improve treatment.

Our research programme is expanding and currently includes studies of drug resistance in breast cancer, Parkinson's disease, vitamin C and stomach cancer, blood vessel growth in disease, AIDS and neurological damage, a new scanner to study brain function, and sunscreen testing without animals.

© Dr Hadwen Trust
September, 1994

Alternatives

From the Research for Health Charities Group

The law in the UK says that animals cannot be used if there is any other way that the medical research work can be carried out.

- Some people say that we should never use animals in medical research because there are always other methods which are better.
- A few people say that doctors only use animals because they like causing pain and cutting things up.
- Doctors are often criticised for using animals in medical research by people who do not do any research themselves.
- A very few people say that all of our medical progress has been made by studying people, or by improving diet, sanitation and education, and that animal studies have not helped at all.

- Many of the techniques which do not need to use animals in medical research have been developed by the medical charities.
- Some people say that they would prefer not to use animals, but that at the moment research work still needs to be done using live animals.
- Some people think that doctors should not do unnecessary experiments, or ones which have been done before.
- Some people think that only sick animals or humans should be used in experiments, and that it is not fair to use healthy ones.
- Some people say that you should not give money to charities which fund medical research using animals, and that you should give money to welfare charities instead.

- Nearly all doctors and many animal welfare organisations say that animal studies have been very important in understanding diseases and finding treatments.
- The medical charities say they would eventually like to stop using animals. They do not give grants to researchers if the work can be done without animals, or is not important enough to need their use.
- At some stage in the understanding of diseases, or in looking for a treatment, living systems must be studied. Usually this will mean using both animals and people.
- When doctors have decided how a disease is caused, and developed a possible treatment, the work can continue in human patients.

© The Research for Health Charities Group

The Alternatives

Statements by animals rights groups and animal welfare charities

'Modern non-animal scientific research techniques are proving far more reliable safety testing methods, and if peaceful campaigning is kept up – we are confident that this needless suffering can be phased out by the end of the decade.'

NAVS, Ardrossan & Saltcoats Herald 16.04.93.

'Future medical progress and human safety will not be achieved through animal research. Instead resources must be channelled into more effective methods of direct relevance to people – methods that already exist.'

BUAV leaflet 'One in 3.5 Million' distributed 1992.

'There are humane and more reliable alternatives to animal experiments, such as computed models, molecular research, population research, test tube tissues and micro-organisms.'

BUAV, Northampton Mercury 25.02.93.

'This list contains details of some of the charities which fund research using animals and also details of some of the charities that are not in any way involved with animal experiments. A list such as this provides carefully researched, reliable information to enable those who wish to donate money or time to a charity that is not involved with animal experiments to choose one.'

BUAV, Northampton Mercury 25.02.93.

'We have produced a carefully researched guide listing charities which use animal tests and those that don't.'

BUAV, Western Morning News 26.6.93.

'The use of animal models, because of differences between species, will never be perfectly relevant to man. However, they do often reveal the unexpected. Non-animal methods, in contrast, tend to tell us expected things and are therefore less likely to reveal the complex interactions which appear in a whole organism.'

*FRAME, 'Issues – Animal Experiments'
Hobsons Publishing 1992.*

'All mammals, human or animals, are complex: they contain organs and body systems that interact. Metabolic cycles and blood pressure, for example, simply cannot be duplicated in any way other than with a living creature.'

*FRAME, 'Biology Now'
Hobsons Publishing 1993.*

Statements by doctors, medical research charities and scientists

'The medical research charities all make extensive use of tissue culture, computer modelling, human clinical trials and population studies. We are world leaders in these fields and together with those sponsored by the MRC our researchers have been responsible for most of the major UK advances which have reduced the need for some animals in some research.'

RHCG, Wrexham Leader 24.09.93.

'Naturally improvements in diet, housing and sanitation have made an enormous difference. Our public education programmes will improve the situation in the future, but it is our medical research which has identified the diet and health factors which we can control.'

RHCG, Wrexham Leader 24.09.93.

'. . . it is pointless telling a young child with AIDS, multiple sclerosis, muscular dystrophy, cystic fibrosis, leukaemia, arthritis, heart disease or diabetes that an improved lifestyle will bring a cure.'

RHCG, Wrexham Leader 24.09.93.

'Of the 18 "medical research" charities listed as not using any animals in the 1992 BUAV guide *Health With Humanity*, nine say they do not carry out any medical research at all, two cannot be traced, one raises funds for equipment, one had not started giving grants, one looks at cell structure, and two carry out human clinical research which therefore would not need to use animals. Of the remaining two charities, one genuinely carries out research aimed at promoting alternatives to animal experiments, the other is searching for an early diagnostic test for cancer using human cells, and is deliberately avoiding using animals. All the other 63 registered medical research charities in the UK make some use of animal studies at some point, or build upon the work of others who have done so.'

RHCG, Andover Advertiser, 3.12.93

'Clearly a population study is not an alternative to tissue culture in a test-tube in a laboratory, and a computer model isn't an alternative to looking at patients in hospital with a disease . . . we're looking at five different techniques here, of which tissue culture is one, animal studies is another, for when we need to look in a living system. Ninety-seven percent of the work of my charities is done without using animals.'

RHCG, BBC Radio Derby 17.02.94.

*The above quotes were provided by the Research for Health Charities Group
September, 1994*

Alternatives to animals in research

From the Humane Research Trust

Why are alternatives necessary?

There are many good reasons for finding alternatives to the use of animals in medical research – issues already discussed, such as the morality of using another species to benefit ourselves. Another aspect is how safe animal tested drugs are. Pharmaceutical companies benefit from the public's fear of terrible diseases and offer a sense of security by claiming their products have been safety tested on animals. In reality, this is often far from justified. Drugs are regularly being taken off the market because they prove harmful, even fatal, when used by humans – and these harmful effects had not shown up in animal tests. You need only to read the newspapers to find examples. The list of such drugs is a very long and ever increasing one. Let us take a brief look at some of the scientific reasons why animal testing is flawed.

The safety aspect of animal testing

There are major genetic and physiological differences between human beings and animals which means drugs tested on animals may not react in the same way on humans. Species react differently to each other ('species variation') and it is important to remember animal tests never really show us exactly what will happen in humans. There are some side effects which will never show up in animal tests because animals cannot tell researchers how they are feeling. So side effects such as nausea, headaches depression and dizziness will never be discovered until they are experienced by people.

Animal experiments have been a hindrance not a help to doctors by

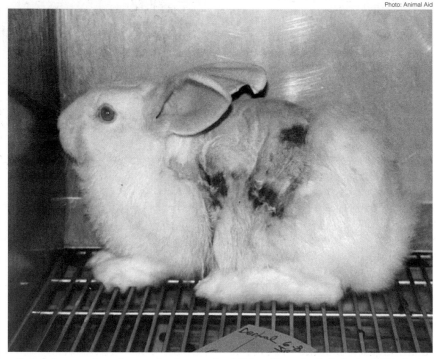

Photo: Animal Aid

Animal experiments reached a peak of 5.6 million in Britain in 1971, but have been falling steadily since 1976 despite an expansion in the scale of laboratory experiments.

producing an almost endless series of misleading results. If doctors had taken proper notice of animal based research, we would be without many useful drugs in wide use today. Progress has been made in medical research *in spite of* not *because of* the use of animals. If, for whatever reason, there were no animals, medical research would not have been impossible. More scientists would simply have been more creative sooner.

Many experiments are very distressing – and still unreliable. A good example of this is the LD50 test Discomfort, fear, frustration, denial of instincts, blunting of natural defence mechanisms in a sterile environment, and diet distortions are just some of the ways in which results can be affected and consequently misleading.

Often to get measurable results massive doses are applied, despite the fact that effect can vary with dosage. Different metabolisms come into effect at different levels of dosage, all of which leads to unclear and inaccurate results. Diseases are given artificially to animals in laboratories and these will never be the same as diseases which develop spontaneously in humans.

Not only are live animal experiments slow and expensive, they are unreliable too. This deficiency in reliability gives rise to what are known as 'false positives' and 'false negatives'.

A *false positive* is when a drug would be deemed as unsafe because of animal tests, yet is of great value to man. Consequently, false positives can deprive us of really valuable drugs.

A *false negative* is when a drug is classed as safe because of the results of animal testing, but then proves to be harmful to man. Consequently, false negatives can result in death and deformities.

Unlike many 'false positives', 'false nega-tives' do become known. Both are costly – not only financially, but because of the effect they can have on human health.

Why does vivisection continue?

In view of all these problems, it seems natural to ask, why are animals still used in experimentation?

There are a number of reasons. The vested interests of the pharma-ceutical and chemical companies, the commitment to out of date thinking, the legislation that states drugs must be tested on animals to be deemed 'safe' and commercial businesses who give the public a false sense of security about their products being 'safety tested' on animals. A whole industry thrives on breeding animals and providing cages, food and surgical equipment for experiments. Universities, hospitals and private laboratories carry on being funded as long as they devise new animal experiments. Usable results are not required, just proof that the experi-

ment has been done. By playing on the public's fear of cancer and AIDS amongst other diseases, vivisection can be promoted as the only way in which scientists will ever find solutions to human health problems.

Future generations will find to-day's vivisection practice impossible to understand and be appalled that such experiments were allowed to continue for so long.

It makes sense then to take a good, hard look at the alternatives available to help people and save animals

Humane research

It is only in about the last 30 years or so that serious efforts have been made to find alternatives to using animals in research. Nearly all of this work has been funded by the private and charity sector with the Government contributing very little. Despite the lack of proper funding, *great* advances have been made. It is worth thinking what even greater advances and breakthroughs *would* be made with even better funding.

Animal experiments reached a peak of 5.6 million in Britain in 1971, but have been falling steadily since 1976 despite an expansion in the scale of laboratory experiments. Humane (or alternative) research

methods have made a major con-tribution to this decrease and certain types of experiments on animals have been replaced completely.

The advantages of non-animal research have become apparent. Not only are animals saved from suffering and death in laboratories, but the new techniques have invariably proved more efficient, more accurate and more economical in time and money. As many of these techniques are carried out using human tissue, the results are more directly relevant to human disease than work carried out on animals.

There are alternative tests available now that were thought impossible even ten years ago. Attitudes to humane research have changed rapidly in the last five years. Considerable interest is now being expressed by the scientific community and the growth of public concern about animal experiments is attracting attention to humane alternatives. The outlook holds much potential. It is not enough to say animals cannot be replaced. For the sake of humans and animals we *must* continue the search for sophisticated, reliable and humane methods of medical research.

Worst violence fear as hunting starts

New laws are voted on after clashes with saboteurs increase

By Nicholas Schoon

An ugly little guerrilla war is waged in the English countryside through each autumn winter and spring. It is an affair of deep fear and loathing, split lips and black eyes, chases and ambushes as hunt saboteurs clash with hunting folk on horseback and their followers on foot.

With the opening of the new season three weeks off there are fears that this year's could be uglier than ever.

Some 3,000 regular saboteurs will be disrupting 50 of Britain's 340 hunt meetings each week says their spokesman Ben Ponton.

Usually, the worst damage done is cuts requiring stitches, concussion and a few days in hospital. But the conflict killed someone last year and may well do so again. Thomas Worby aged 15 was crushed by a horsebox with the Cambridgeshire Foxhounds as he attempted to decouple it from a vehicle during a hunt near St Neots.

Thomas who attended a home for children with behavioural difficulties was with saboteurs from Milton Keynes who are known in field sport circles for being particularly dedicated and disruptive.

They target several hunts but the one singled out for most disruption is the Bicester Hunt with Whaddon Chase – an amalgamation of two hunts.

It is fairly large, rides four times a week and is known for some celebrated members and guest riders including Michael Heseltine's wife, Anne, Baroness Mallalieu, a Labour spokeswoman in the Lords, and John

Mortimer's wife Penny, are also members. Together they are trying to make Labour tolerate hunting.

Among saboteurs this hunt – the BHWC – is well known for fighting back. From Milton Keynes, Toni Gellard and her boyfriend Stephen Price, leading activists in the Three Shires Hunt Saboteurs, regularly set out to confront the BHWC.

A week ago she was confronted herself with a minor explosion under her Peugeot car parked outside her home near the town centre. A small box-shaped device produced a loud bang, flames and large quantities of

smoke. First the fire brigade and then the army bomb squad attended while police cordoned off the estate.

Ms Gellard, 23, says a spent shotgun cartridge was thrown in her garden a few days before the incident, and afterwards fuses were removed from the fusebox outside her front door. She believes she is being warned off by hunt supporters – a claim the BHWC rejects.

'Her allegation is a disgrace and we condemn the placing of this device,' said Robert Vallence, its secretary. 'It's made me angry but it's not going to put me off sabbing,' said Ms Gellard.

She admits she and her colleagues fight back when cornered, although they have sometimes telephoned the police for help. 'We

Photo: British Field Sports Society

Some 3,000 regular saboteurs will be disrupting 50 of Britain's 340 hunt meetings each week.

WE'VE GIVEN UP FOXES – NOW WE'RE HUNTING HUNT SABOTEURS!

STOP THE HUNT

Ken Pyne

used to be passive but now we stick up for ourselves,' she said. 'A lot of us do carry sticks – you would use them if necessary.'

'Sabbing' has brought her into conflict with the law. She was bound over to keep the peace last year and is now facing a charge of Actual Bodily Harm after an incident involving a woman hunter on horseback. She will plead not guilty.

The BHWC, like several hunts which face repeated sabotage has organised stewards to monitor the saboteurs. These men and women are drawn from the foot followers and they tail the saboteurs' vans in Land Rovers and video-record them. They can also legally remove them using minimum force from land on which they are trespassing after giving them three warnings.

Members of the BHWC and other hunts find the press and public perception of the conflict almost as infuriating as the sabotage. This is not a battle over the morality of fox-hunting but of the rule of law in the countryside they say. They are following a traditional and completely legal rural pursuit. The saboteurs are urban fanatics who march on to land they do not own and break laws of trespass as well as ruining their fun and endangering them.

The Earl of Yarborough hunts several times a week with the Brockelsby Hunt in Lincolnshire and was attacked in his car on the way to a meet two weeks ago. He said: 'There have been so many incidents of abuse,

threats and violence – we are getting fed up and very angry. He cites threats to burn down houses and the wielding of a broken bottle. 'I'm certainly not going to stop,' he said. 'We've been hunting here for 400 years. But you wonder how much abuse people can take.'

Huntsmen concede that their on-foot followers who are 'at the thick end of it all' have been caught up in more violence because they say saboteurs are more skilled at provoking punch-ups. 'They go for the young farmers whom it's easier to set off,' said one. The use of stewards with a mandate to remove trespassers has also raised the potential for violence.

The BHWC's record is not spotless. One of its kennelmen, Michael Smith, and hunt marshal Richard Cheshire were each jailed for two months last year after a well-known saboteur was pushed into the path of a four-wheel 'quad' motorcycle and injured.

Both sides have unpleasant tales to tell of finding themselves heavily outnumbered then kicked and beaten

---

The police have become increasingly frequent visitors at hunt meetings as the sabotage and violence has escalated

---

on some quiet rural byway by 'thugs'. Both sides say they will never surrender. Two weeks ago a young Somerset farmer, Tom Osborne of the Mendip Farmers Foxhounds, was set upon by several saboteurs on his land near Wells. Acid was sprayed in his eyes and he was hit on the head with a stick studded with tacks. He fell unconscious, bleeding heavily, and spent several days in hospital.

That same day three hunt observers from the League Against Cruel Sports – who do not take part in sabotage – were attacked by followers of that hunt said Kevin Saunders of the League. 'They were all bashed in the face and had thick lips.'

All this has been taking place during the prelims – the cub-hunting season when small patches of woodland are surrounded by huntsmen and the young inexperienced hounds sent in with a few veteran dogs to seek out cubs.

The police have become increasingly frequent visitors at hunt meetings as the sabotage and violence has escalated. But once the Criminal Justice Bill is enacted in the next few weeks their presence may become much more obvious. The Bill effectively makes hunt sabotage a crime rather than a matter of trespass and the huntsmen are pinning their hopes on the Co-stabulary to re-establish law and order in the countryside. It is not a task they relish. © *The Independent on Sunday October, 1994*

The real animals

Hunt saboteurs claim that their tactics against country sports supporters are non-violent. Year by year, month by month, this is shown to be false. Information from British Field Sports Society

Similar claims that saboteurs will not intimidate, terrify or injure animals are also made, but the simple truth is that the harassment and violence so often vented on people in the hunting field is also directed against animals. Horses and hounds have been injured, even killed, as a result of standard tactics used by saboteurs.

Hounds and horses beaten

Saboteurs frequently carry staves made of iron or wood. Some of these have been fitted with sharp nails. A favoured practice is grabbing a horse by its reins and hitting the flanks with a stick. The Hunt Saboteurs Association magazine shows how to make a whip. Although not actually advocated, hounds and horses are thrashed with home-made whips.

- In March 1990 a hound in Surrey received severe head injuries as a result of being beaten by saboteurs.
- In 1992 two saboteurs in Essex were bound over to keep the peace after thrashing hounds.

- In Kent in October 1993, horses were beaten and riders attacked.
- Hounds from the Surrey Union Hunt have been so terrified that some now refuse to leave the hound lorry when saboteurs are present.

Hunt followers are sometimes rammed at high speed by saboteurs' vehicles. The incidents are neither new nor infrequent:

- In 1982, a horse required thirty stitches to its flank after a saboteur had driven into hounds and horses in Leicestershire. The saboteur was banned from driving for three months.

Drawing hounds onto roads and railways

Howl, the magazine of the Hunt Saboteurs Association states that 'good hunt sabotage depends upon the interference with the huntman's control of the pack.' Fake calls on hunting horns, hollowing and shouting are persistently used by saboteurs.

Although discouraged by *Howl*, the fact is that saboteurs recklessly draw hounds onto busy roads creating a danger to the animals and to road users.

Since 1991, saboteurs have used tape recordings of a pack of hounds in full cry. These are played from loudspeakers on the top of cars. By definition, they are on roads, deliberately drawing hounds out of control and into danger.

On other occasions, hounds are drawn onto railway lines. On Boxing Day 1993, an unidentified saboteur drew a hound onto the railway in Somerset. It was killed by an Intercity train before the hunt were able to rescue it.

Irritant sprays

Claims by saboteurs that sprays are used as scent-dullers on the ground, and contain simple 'Anti-Mate' or a citronella mix, are false. The sprays often contain powerful irritants.

The Manchester Analytical Laboratories examined one such spray: 'The liquid would have a

An injured policeman receives attention from his colleagues. 150 saboteurs attacked police, hunt supporters and stewards. Five police officers and a hunt steward were injured.

somewhat irritating effect when applied to an animal's coat. It would be extremely painful if it was being sprayed into an animal's eyes.'

It had been sprayed directly at hounds.

- In December 1991 ten hounds in Norfolk needed veterinary treatment when saboteurs sprayed substances into their eyes.
- In 1988 furniture polish was sprayed at a hound's face in Wales.
- Other hunts regularly report that their hounds need treatment when sprayed by saboteurs.
- In January and November 1993, when hunt supporters were taken to hospital as a result of being sprayed by saboteurs, the substances were found to be ammonia.

General cruelty

Constant evidence of cruelty to animals by saboteurs is demonstrated not only against hunting, but also against other country sports:

- Glass and nails were found strewn over a coursing field before the Waterloo Cup in February 1981. Greyhounds could have been badly cut.
- A saboteur kicked a labrador at a shoot in Lancashire in October 1993.
- Hidden wire was placed across gates and fences at a hunt in Cambridgeshire in November 1993, a potential death trap for horses and riders.

- Three thunder flashes were let off, terrifying horses and hounds in Hampshire in November 1993. Smoke flares are listed as useful for disruption in the Hunt Saboteurs Association Tactics Booklet.
- One hound was stolen from a Buckinghamshire hunt on New Year's Day 1994. It has since been recovered but has been spayed and had an ear mutilated.
- A hound was beaten to death in Wales with a hammer in November 1993.
- In 1988 a hound in Surrey was beaten to death with a spade.

Who, then, are the real animals?

Video takes field sports campaign into schools

The British Field Sports Society is to distribute an educational pack to 20,000 schools in an effort to 'put the record straight' about the role of field sports in preserving the countryside

The material, which includes a video entitled *The Balance of Nature* and a teacher's handbook, will be sent to schools free of charge in the hope it will be incorporated in lessons.

Children between the ages of 11 and 16 who attend urban schools will be encouraged to consider the implications of farming and country sports on the countryside and its environment.

According to the society, material distributed by the RSPCA and anti-field sports organisations is already used in schools and should be balanced by another point of view.

By Dan Conaghan

But the BFSS director, Mr Peter Voute, said he was aware that some schools were 'anti' field sports and children of gamekeepers, ghillies and field sportsmen sometimes suffered intimidation from fellow pupils and teachers.

He cited one child's experience when her teacher misunderstood the practice of 'beating' to raise game birds from a moor. When the girl pointed out that the birds were not actually beaten but simply flushed out, she was given a black mark.

Mr Voute said: 'We have a huge educational job ahead of us. The video and the other material is stage one. The next stage is to get children out into the countryside so they can see how field sports work first hand.'

He added that the countryside was 'threatened by misunderstanding', something he hoped would be reversed by the BFSS's efforts .

The BFSS showed the video to children and two teachers at a press conference in London yesterday. The film showed a year in the country and sports such as mink hunting, grouse shooting and deer stalking. The commentary pointed out that land which was managed to accommodate game often preserved the natural habitat of other wildlife.

Mrs Gail Branch, a junior school teacher from Lancashire, said she had no experience of field sports and neither had most of the children she taught. 'I do think this project is worthwhile,' she said. 'It is important for children to be shown a balanced argument. On television you only usually see demos by anti-bloodsports people.'

Her daughter, Rachel, 13, said her school friends had little knowledge about the countryside and rarely visited it. 'The video tells you a lot about it, which was interesting. I think people should go and see the countryside, too, and make up their own mind about the sports.'

'The next stage is to get children out into the countryside so they can see how field sports work first hand'

Other children also found the video thought-provoking. Nick Mather, 12, said his school studies covered plants and wildlife but rarely tackled field sports. He was sympathetic to the BFSS view that gamekeeping plays a role in conserving the countryside .

'The video shows field sports aren't all bad and about killing things,' he said. 'You've got to protect the countryside too,' he said. 'I can see why you have to kill some foxes to keep the numbers down and rabbits to keep crops safe.'

Victoria van Terheyden, 13, whose mother works for the BFSS, thought other children who were 'madly in love' with all animals might not realise that some of them can do damage.

She said: 'If some foxes weren't hunted there are lots of other animals who wouldn't stand a chance and get eaten. I thought it was good video and I didn't know about deer hunting until I saw it.'

The BFSS plans to organise coach trips to show the countryside to children from urban areas. These would include visits to hunt kennels, farms and shoots around the country.

Thugs, wreckers and bullies

The truth about hunt violence. Information from Hunt Saboteurs

Lies, damn lies and green wellies

In the past three years, the hunting community has realised it has a serious image problem and has put substantial effort and millions of pounds into trying to make themselves more acceptable. Much of this effort has consisted of a smear campaign co-ordinated by the British Field Sports Society (BFSS) to cover up the brutality and violence of hunt supporters by 'exposing' saboteurs as class war militants bent on violence and destruction. There is precious little evidence to support this theory, but the hardy folk of the hunting community will not let such trivia deter them and simply make up their 'proof'. Their campaign of smears has met with some success – solely on the basis of the sort of ill-founded propaganda exposed below, the Home Secretary has introduced new legislation to jail saboteurs for caring about animals.

'Saboteurs have attacked or caused injury to horses and hounds, giving the lie to their claim that they are animal lovers'

Not true. In fact, hunts are wildly reckless in their treatment of their own animals and saboteurs often have to intervene to save the animals from injury. At the Portman Hunt in November 1993, a panic-stricken horse found itself neck-deep in near-freezing water after its rider tried to

Photo: League Against Cruel Sports

force it to jump a river which was plainly too big. A female saboteur who was trained in caring for animals tried to help the horse, by now collapsing, as members of the hunt stood around watching. The rider immediately ignored his horse's plight and turned on the girl, knocking her to the ground and then leaping on her, punching her in the face repeatedly. When the horse was eventually rescued with the saboteur's help, the rider apologised and admitted he should not have attempted the jump or attacked the girl who had only wanted to help an animal in distress.

'Saboteurs recklessly draw hounds onto busy roads . . . On other occasions, hounds are drawn onto railway lines.'

Not true. Hunters regularly trespass on roads and railway lines in their pursuit of hunted creatures and then try to blame saboteurs for their own stupidity. For example, in July 1992 the Avon Vale Foxhunt lost control of their hounds on a busy road and a hound was killed. No saboteurs were present, yet the hunt accused a local saboteur of calling the hound into the road. He was over 15 miles away at the time. In contrast, the Spooners & West Dartmoor Foxhunt were honest enough to admit their failings when their hounds ran riot across the A386 near Yelverton in March 1992. Only prompt intervention by saboteurs saved both hounds and members of the public from injury. Hunt Master Charles Doughty said 'The saboteurs could not have been nicer . . . (They) blew their horns beautifully to get the hounds out of danger and back to us.'

'Recruiting posters, recovered from a campus, which offered payment of £30 a day plus lunch.' (for hunt saboteurs)

Not true. This story, which appeared in *The Field*, is just one of many published over the years claiming that saboteurs are a paid rent-a-mob. Despite frequent challenges to produce evidence to back up their claims, the hunting community have been unable to do so, because they are simply not true. In private, even

Saboteurs come from all backgrounds, age groups, professions and political points of view.

they are prepared to admit that saboteurs are motivated by genuine concern for animals rather than financial gain. As Stephen Loveridge, BFSS press officer, admitted in a letter in January 1994: 'We know full well that there is no evidence that saboteurs are paid, and I am sure that they are not.'

'These people are not interested in the welfare of the foxes, their targets are people who hunt. It is nothing more than anarchist class warfare.'

Not true. We regard the issue of class as entirely irrelevant to the central moral issue of cruelty. Saboteurs come from all backgrounds, age groups, professions and political points of view. On the other side of the coin, the worst perpetrators of cruelty and violence at hunts are terriermen who are solidly working class. So called class struggle is deliberately used to cloud the issue and provide a handy diversion for hunters unable to defend themselves on moral grounds to spread alarm about 'sinister political extremists'. Perhaps they mean people like the now-famous 'Granny Group' of saboteurs in Surrey? Every one of this brave group of senior citizens is over 60 and there's not a mohican, among them. Unfortunately this does not seem to exempt them from violent attacks by hunt thugs. Or perhaps the hunt lobby mean such

notorious class warriors as Rev. Bert Jones, a 65 year-old church minister, who has been a hunt saboteur for three years.

Similarly, the word terrorist is frequently flung about in an attempt to smear genuine animal lovers, often coupled with lurid tales of bomb attacks. In June 1990, hunt supporter John Newberry-Street gained much valuable anti-saboteur publicity when a nail-bomb was found under his Land Rover. Further investigation revealed that he had planted the bomb himself and he later told police, 'I did it to discredit the animal rights saboteurs'. He was jailed for nine months for his bomb hoax and asked for several other similar offences to be taken into account.

'A leading protester was Ms Jo Harris (a "peaceful activist" with a recent court conviction for assault) . . .'
(BFSS press release after female-only protest at the Hursley Hambledon Foxhunt 1994)

Not true. Ms Harris in fact has no criminal record at all, but this smear seems to be an attempt to detract attention from a series of sexual attacks by local hunt thugs. These include a particularly serious attack, when a six-strong gang of hunt supporters attempted to drag her into woodland, boasting loudly that they were going to gang-rape her.
© *Hunt Saboteurs Association, November, 1994*

The League Against Cruel Sports

The League's five approaches to the abolition of bloodsports

1 The League campaigns for Parliamentary legislation to protect wild animals from cruelty. This will also ensure that the hunting of wildlife with packs of dogs in the name of sport will become illegal. Parliament has already taken action to protect animals with the 1911 Protection of Animals Act (1912 in Scotland) which makes it an offence to inflict unnecessary suffering on domestic and captive animals. Wild animals are excluded from this legal protection and therefore hunting is allowed to continue. Clearly this is an anomaly that should be rectified.

Outlawing the infliction of unnecessary suffering on wild animals would not prevent genuine pest control operations. Fox, deer and hare hunting with hounds is conducted purely for sport and not for pest control. This is because all hunting with hounds is inefficient by design, in the interests of providing sport for those who participate. The hounds are bred not for their speed, which would produce a quick kill, but rather for the stamina that ensures a long chase. Various scientific reports and opinion polls clearly show that the fox is not a significant pest in the countryside.

The role of the League is to provide MPs, local councillors and political parties with clear factual information about wildlife protection and why the hunting of wild animals with dogs should be abolished. The progress in gaining support for our campaign within Parliament has been remarkable over the last few years. It is not uncommon for over 200 MPs to sign Early Day Motions calling for the abolition of stag hunting or hare coursing. The 1990-1991 session of Parliament saw a number of wildlife protection Bills

To date over 120 local councils have banned hunting on land that they own or control.

introduced into the House of Commons. These included Bills to abolish hare coursing, deer hunting, fox-hunting, and to close loopholes in the 1973 Badgers' Act, to protect badger setts and give further protection to the badger itself. The legislative proposals in defence of badgers were successful. It is clear that in the 1990s the minority that delight in hunting and killing wild animals for sport will find themselves increasingly isolated.

Parliament is now ready to legislate on the issue of wildlife cruelty and the League believes that a majority of MPs, given a free vote, would support genuine protection for wildlife. All that is now required is a government that will allow the Parliament time to fully consider a Bill to protect wild animals.

Another aspect of the political campaign can be seen in the support gained from local authorities all over the country. To date over 120 local councils have banned hunting on land that they own or control. Over half the county councils in the country have a policy opposing hunting and thousands of acres owned by local authorities are no longer permitted to be used for hunting.

2 The League's Public Relations and Press Departments provide information public and the media and raise revenue to fund all aspects of our work. We respond to thousands of requests every year from television companies, radio stations and from newspapers requesting further information and photographs about hunting and the campaign to ensure the abolition of these activities. League staff, representatives and supporters visit schools and many social and political organisations in order to speak about the League's work. The League also produces videos about the different aspects of hunting and these are sent to organisations and schools when a speaker is not available. The Fund Raising Officer publicises our work and encourages members and supporters of the League to contribute to our campaigns.

3 It is important to obtain scientific evidence to present factual information to those who will make the decisions about the management of wildlife. Therefore we have funded independent scientific reports and published the results. A recent project funded by the League was undertaken by Dr. Ray Hewson of Aberdeen University. The study looked into fox predation on lambs and the findings have been published by the League in a document entitled *The Fox – Victim of Myth*. The report clearly shows that, even in the most difficult areas for the fox's survival and in the absence of control, it is still not a significant pest to farmers. In 1990 the League published a document from information gathered by the National Federation of Badger Groups, entitled *The Case for the Protection of Badger Setts*. This was presented to all MPs discussing the Protection of Badger Setts Bill and helped ensure the Bill's success. A highly critical report on falconry has also been published by the League.

4 The League owns and controls over 2,000 acres of sanctuary land covering 38 different sites in the West Country. Land acquisitions are restricted to the Devon and Somerset area in order that our wildlife sanctuaries can be properly and effectively managed. We hold annual Open Days for members and supporters of the League who wish to see how the sanctuaries are run. The land is purchased to protect wildlife. Rare flora also receives protection within our sanctuaries. All hunting is banned on the League sanctuaries. League staff organise work parties of volunteers to undertake conservation work on these important areas of protected countryside.

5 In certain cases legal services are offered to League members who have suffered problems with their local hunt. Free advice is given on trespass, livestock worrying, hound entry, crop damage or any other difficulty. The League deals with numerous legal actions during the course of each hunting season for trespass and damage. We also offer legal advice on how to prevent a hunt entering onto prohibited land.

© *League Against Cruel Sports*
December, 1994

Foxes and fox-hunting

From the League Against Cruel Sports

Is the fox a pest ?
Each spring when fox-cubs are born, the fox population of Britain may reach half a million individuals. It is obvious that if foxes were a serious threat to agriculture half a million of them would cause devastation and havoc. The fact is that most of the fox's feeding habits are not detrimental to farming – on the contrary, their predation on rabbits, rats and voles, all of which are considerable pests on the 70% of farmland given over to arable production, is of positive benefit to the farmer. Foxes also eat earthworms, insects, beetles, and fallen fruit as well as usefully scavenging the carcases of wild and domestic animals and birds.

With around 98% of poultry confined in intensive farming systems, it must be a rare fox which ever gets the opportunity to taste chicken but they will take advantage

---

Fox-hunting has the same purpose as the now illegal pastimes of dog-fighting, bear baiting and cock-fighting – to provide amusement for human beings

---

of badly housed poultry and have very occasionally been known to steal free-range hens in daylight. However, the provision of sound night roosting sheds for the birds and a little electric fencing is usually enough to prevent such problems.

According to the Ministry of Agriculture, predation on lambs by foxes is 'insignificant'. Studies show that even by farmers' estimates, only one in two hundred lambs falls victim to a fox, whereas between 10% and 24% of lambs die from hypothermia, malnutrition or disease, or are still-born. Foxes carry away such casualties and are often seen in the lambing fields hoping to scavenge afterbirth. Because of this, foxes are ideal scapegoats for bad husbandry or lazy shepherds.

Foxes must have a year long supply of food, so it follows that scavenging at lambing time would not affect the overall fox population density.

If a fox (often known as a 'rogue') does become a nuisance to a farmer, the animal can be selectively shot or caught in a humane cage-trap. However, it is better to protect vulnerable stock rather than to kill foxes, because if a vacuum occurs other foxes will simply move in to fill it.

29

Fox-hunting

Fox-hunting has the same purpose as the now illegal pastimes of dog-fighting, bear baiting and cock-fighting – to provide amusement for human beings. It is not a form of fox control, nor is it meant to be. The 'control' argument was recently invented to counter the protests of those of us to whom the killing of animals for amusement is morally unacceptable .

Foxes mate in January and cubs are born in the spring. Fox-hunting continues through the winter into April and occasionally even May. It is obvious therefore that not only pregnant and nursing vixens are hunted and killed, but also the dog-fox, on whom the vixen and cubs often rely for food. Every year, thousands of fox-cubs are orphaned this way and many die of starvation or are picked up and taken to animal shelters.

Fox-hunters block up earths and badger setts the night before the hunt to ensure that foxes are forced to run until exhausted. Fox-hounds are specially bred to run more slowly than the fox, but they can sustain a prolonged chase; accordingly the fox can outrun the hound until it is exhausted and the bigger and stronger hounds are then able to catch it. The longer the fox can keep up its efforts, the more so-called 'sport' is obtained; therefore a weak, elderly or pregnant fox provides only a short hunt. A young, fit and strong fox can last up to two hours before it succumbs to fatigue, but the hounds can run for six or seven hours if necessary. If fast running dogs such as greyhounds or lurchers were used to hunt foxes, the whole thing would be over in seconds, but then there would be no 'sport'.

Foxes are not a natural prey species and have never suffered predation as a governing factor on their population density. The distress suffered by a prey species must be considerable when pursued by a predator but the trauma must be far greater for a fox not naturally adapted to endure long periods of pursuit.

Even if the fox manages to find an unblocked earth or badger sett in which to hide, the 'sportsmen' will either 'evict' the terrified quarry with terriers so that it can be hunted again or if it is too exhausted to 'bolt', the terriers keep it under attack until the hunt servants and terrier men can dig it out and kill it. The death itself though violent and painful may be

Fox, deer and hare hunting with hounds is conducted purely for sport and not for pest control.

relatively quick. However the real cruelty of fox-hunting lies in the exhaustion, terror and trauma inflicted on the victim.

Fox ecology

The fox, like all predators in nature, has its numbers governed by the availability of food and the establishment and defence of territories. Man kills many tens of thousands of foxes annually, but vixens produce enough cubs to bring the numbers back to the density appropriate to the availability of food and territory. Fox killing merely produces an unnaturally young fox population; the actual numbers of foxes remain the same.

A survey carried out by Dr Stephen Harris of Bristol University in 1987 revealed that fox-hunts kill between 12,000 and 13,000 foxes a year. Dr Harris points out that this may represent only 2.5% of the fox population, whereas fox populations can survive an annual mortality rate of up to 70% and still recover. Dr Harris concluded that, *'It is clear that fox-hunts play no significant role in the control of fox populations.'* In other words, 12,000 foxes die annually for no other reason than 'sport'.

Left alone by man, fox populations will be higher in areas of abundance of food and lower where food is scarce. This can be seen in towns and cities, where large numbers of foxes survive on refuse and high rodent populations. A 3-year study by Aberdeen University showed that in the absence of any form of fox control, there was neither an increase in fox numbers or in the number of lambs lost.

Foxes form stable family groups which defend their own territory against intruding foxes, and which will reproduce at a similar rate to their fatalities. The fox population would therefore not explode if all methods of fox killing were suspended. Surplus fox-cubs, usually dog-foxes, leave the home range when mature and seek to form or join new family groups in vacant territories. Most will be quickly accepted into groups depleted by perhaps a road accident, or human predation, while others may spend a considerable period as 'itinerants' before finding a new territory.

Fox-hunting: let's take action

From the RSPCA

Foxes have been hunted for sport in Britain throughout the past 250 years. As people have become increasingly concerned about animal welfare over the past century, so hunt followers have given various reasons for their pursuit, besides the fact that they enjoy it.

Today, when pressed to justify their actions, most hunt supporters explain that killing foxes by hunting them with hounds is necessary to protect poultry and livestock, and makes a positive contribution to conservation. They say that the fox is a pest whose numbers have to be controlled.

Despite all the changes there have been in agriculture, in the environment and in our knowledge of fox biology, the hunt supporters' arguments have not altered.

The RSPCA rejects those arguments

We say that:
- Fox-hunting is NOT necessary for the protection of livestock.
- Fox-hunting is NOT necessary for conservation.
- As research has shown, the fox is NOT a significant pest.

But our main objection is that *considerable suffering* is inflicted on foxes chased and killed by dogs for 'sport'. After 250 years, it is time for fox hunting to stop.

The fox and farm livestock

This century has seen a marked change in attitudes to wildlife, and today a more enlightened and tolerant view is taken of many animals once widely regarded as pests. Though the fox has traditionally been thought of as one of them, research over the past 20 years has cast it in a different light.

For example, scientific studies in many parts of the country have shown that foxes kill very few lambs. They do, however, scavenge carcasses of stillborn lambs, or lambs which have died from various causes. It appears, therefore, that the fox is often mistakenly accused of killing lambs.

The fox is often blamed, too, for killing chickens. But today most birds are housed and so at little risk from foxes, while free-range poultry can be protected by suitable fencing.

As far as control of the fox *population* is concerned, there is growing evidence that, in family groups of foxes, only one dominant vixen gives birth, so reproduction is naturally suppressed. Non-selective control methods like hunting disrupt such social mechanisms.

Occasionally an individual fox may be a serious nuisance, and humane destruction of that animal may be necessary. But the RSPCA does not believe that hunting – by nature indiscriminate – is an appropriate method of dealing with a particular animal.

Nor do we believe that it is efficient or humane. If it were intended to be, Foxhounds would be bred for speed rather than stamina, to produce sprinting ability rather than the staying power required for a protracted chase.

The fox and conservation

When fox-hunting began as an organised sport in the early 18th century, the English countryside looked quite different from the way it does now. Hunting people rode to hounds across open ground.

Then the land began to be enclosed by hedges and fences in the interests of agriculture, and the countryside became what it is today. So the hunt followers adapted to the land, and rode instead over fields and hedges.

31

Preservation of coverts, woodland and other uncultivated ground has only ever been an incidental contribution of the hunt to conservation. It has never been its purpose.

Sometimes hunt supporters suggest that as well as conserving the land they are helping to conserve foxes, too, a claim which contradicts their more frequent assertion that foxes are pests which need to be controlled.

The fox and public opinion

In 1978, a National Opinion Poll showed that 60 per cent of the population were in favour of a law to ban fox-hunting. Two subsequent Gallup Poll surveys showed that the figure had risen to 70 per cent in 1984, and to 79 per cent in 1991.

Public opinion can, therefore, change quickly, but the opinions of hunting people seem not to change at all. Their pleasure of 250 years in the pursuit and killing of a wild animal with dogs for sport continues, despite the opposition of nearly three quarters of the people of this country.

Let's take action

If you are opposed to fox-hunting, you can help the RSPCA to bring it to an end. Please write to your MP demanding a change in the law to abolish fox-hunting now.

The RSPCA was founded in 1824 to promote kindness and prevent cruelty to animals. At that time abuse of animals was common.

Since then the RSPCA has achieved much in many areas of animal welfare, but our modern way of life poses its own problems for animals. Their well-being demands the vigilant concern and protection of the Society as much now as ever before.

Today the RSPCA works with equal commitment in four main areas – Companion Animals, Farm Animals, Animal Experimentation and Wild Animals – and because it receives no State aid, relies on the generosity and goodwill of caring people everywhere.

If you would like to make a donation to the RSPCA, or to find out more about becoming a financial supporter or an adult or junior member, or to receive a publications catalogue, see address details on page 39.

Hunting – the facts

From the British Field Sports Society

Is hunting cruel?

In order to answer the question, 'Is hunting cruel?', one must first define cruelty. The Scott Henderson Committee considered cruelty to be 'an act causing unnecessary suffering'.

There is no doubt that the fox population has to be controlled, and hunting with hounds is not only effective, but is also the method which involves the least cruelty. A fox which is hunted by a pack of hounds is either killed instantly, or escapes entirely uninjured.

A popular myth is that the fox is killed by being torn apart by a pack of hounds when it is still alive. This is not true.

On average a foxhound weighs between sixty and seventy five pounds, which makes it four or five times heavier than a fox. A fox is nearly always killed by a single bite to the back of the neck from just one foxhound's powerful jaws. This is irrespective of the number of hounds which might be in pursuit.

After a fox has been killed, the Huntsman will often allow the pack to eat the corpse, but this is after the fox is dead.

Unlike those dogs which pursue their quarry by sight, fox hounds follow the scent of a fox – an invisible, intangible thread which hangs in the air or lies on the ground. They pick up the scent some time after the fox has been around, and for most of the pursuit are out of the fox's sight and hearing. Until the final stages, a fox is often quite unconcerned that it is being pursued at all.

As the Scott Henderson Report put it:

'We are not satisfied that wild animals suffer from apprehension or the after-effects of fear to the same extent as human beings. Wild animals must live very largely in the present, and although a hunted fox, for example, may be aware that it is being hunted and that if the hounds catch it something to be avoided will happen, we think that it would be going beyond the evidence to say that the fox realises that it may be killed.'

The Report continued:

'We think, therefore, that, while it is reasonable to assume that wild animals suffer from temporary fear and terror, there are no grounds for supposing that they suffer from apprehension to the same extent as human beings or that a frightening experience has the same serious or lasting effect upon them as it may have upon us.'

Even when it does realise that it is being followed, a fox will behave with great calm, almost to the point of indifference. It is certainly not terrified. Remember, this is a creature which is not itself in fear of predation. If it has been hunted by hounds before, it escaped unhurt. It has no reason to believe that it has anything to fear.

The majority of people who live in the countryside clearly believe, as evidenced by their public support of hunting and all its associated activities such as point-to-points and pony clubs, that the practice of fox-hunting, controlled and under proper scrutiny, is the most acceptable method of controlling the fox population. Virtually all of these people keep and care about animals. It is difficult to accept that, in their hundreds of thousands, they would countenance, let alone actively support, anything which involved wanton cruelty.

And their support was borne out by the Scott Henderson Committee: 'So far as general cruelty is concerned, we are satisfied that there is less cruelty in fox-hunting than in most other methods of control. For that reason, and in view of the undisputed necessity for the control of foxes, we think that hunting should be allowed to continue. It is a necessary method of control, and its abolition would undoubtedly lead to an increase in the use of more cruel methods and, so far as we can judge, would be resented by the majority of the rural population.'

And key amongst the rural population are the farmers. It is they who allow the hunt to cross their land freely, for they appreciate the role which it plays in managing the fox population. The hunt is at all times responsive to their wishes.

A farmer who has experienced particular problems with foxes will often ask the hunt to kill a certain fox or to break up a group of foxes.

If a hunted fox goes to ground in a natural earth, the strictly enforced rules of the governing body of foxhunting expressly prohibit the digging of the fox from the earth and continuing to hunt it. Nevertheless, a farmer will often insist that the fox, having been located by the hunt, is killed. Under such circumstances, trained staff who follow the hunt on foot are instructed to establish the whereabouts of the fox, to dig down to it, and to dispatch it instantly

Illustration: British Field Sports Society

with a humane killer usually a small pistol fired at point blank range.

These men will often use terriers to hold the fox at bay in a particular part of the earth. They go about their necessary work with all haste, and the fox is quickly destroyed.

Farmers also expect families of foxes to be reduced in number and/or dispersed. This usually happens in the autumn, and the practice is called Autumn Hunting or Cubhunting. The word cub is something of a misnomer. These are families of foxes which may be in their first year, but have normally reached maturity.

At this time of year cattle are still out in the fields, and some crops have yet to be harvested. The hunt may therefore encircle a piece of woodland, into which foxhounds will be directed. The hounds and any foxes they find are encouraged to stay within the woodland, with two objectives.

The first is to ensure that a number of foxes are killed or dispersed. Dispersal results because those foxes which successfully break from cover scatter in all directions.

The second is to develop the young hounds which have joined the pack during the summer. They have important lessons to learn. They must be taught to distinguish between, for

example, foxes and deer, and only to hunt foxes; to know the sound of the horn and what the various calls mean. The huntsman uses his horn and his voice to communicate with his hounds in the way that a shepherd gives instructions to a sheepdog. The close constraints of a piece of woodland enable the huntsman to control the younger hounds and in this way to teach them.

The importance of hunting to conservation

The British countryside is a man–made scene, not a natural one. Our rich heritage of fauna and flora has survived better than any European country because of the love and dedication of generations of country people. For centuries country sports have been played a central role in the process.

We can justly claim that many of the beautiful features of our landscape – the woods, spinneys, hedges, fields, lakes, streams, ponds, moors and heaths – are fashioned and preserved by the pattern of country sports.

As tens of thousands of country people contemplate a bleak future for agriculture, it is vital that all leisure and sporting activities rooted in the countryside are preserved.

The Farming and Wildlife Advisory Group recognises that hunting continues to make a significant contribution to conservation:

'The conservation element is inseparable from the provision of hunting . . .'

In the country of the Warwickshire Foxhounds, 55 woodland areas have been planted specifically for the purpose of hunting and of making converts for foxes. Like many hunts, the Warwickshire owns some of these coverts – seven of them together span nearly 150 acres.

The hunt plays a large part in keeping local bridleways open, maintaining hedges and fences, and clearing and managing woodlands. The hunt also encourages traditional laying of hedges and management of coverts, making an attractive habitat of all kinds.

© *The British Field Sports Society November, 1994*

Deer and staghunting

From the League Against Cruel Sports

Deerhunting

Red Deer are hunted by three packs of hounds in the West Country – the Devon and Somerset, Quantock, and Tiverton Staghounds – and in the south the New Forest Buckhounds hunt male fallow deer. The three West Country packs hunt Autumn stags (mature males) from 1st August to 31st October, the hinds (females) from 1st November to the end of February, and Spring stags (young males) from the start of March to the end of April. In the New Forest, the bucks are hunted in September and from November to the end of April. Since 1989, two new packs have been formed to hunt roe bucks in the South West.

Staghunting

The day's hunting starts with a hunt servant known as the harbourer going out to locate a good, strong deer for hunting. Normally the deer will be in a herd and often there will be a number of suitable victims within that herd. The huntsman selects 11-15 of the more experienced hounds, known as tufters. These are used, along with riders wielding whips, to split up the herd until a suitable stag is running on its own or with only a few others. The whole pack will then be let loose to chase the running deer. The deer herd, often consisting largely of hinds and calves, may be terrorised for several hours before this stage is reached . The image the hunt promotes of a single deer being selected and hunted is misleading. Hounds will often change from one deer to another during the day and small groups of individual hounds will leave the pack to hunt other deer on their own. Furthermore, supporters with CB radios, cross-country motorbikes and four-wheel drive vehicles also pursue and harass the deer. Sightings are radioed back to those near the hounds. Hounds

Nationally, each year at least 80,000 deer are killed by shooting.

are bred for stamina, in order to be slower-running to prolong the day's 'sport'. Their ability to sustain a slower pace over many hours tires the deer which, although initially faster, needs frequent rests.

The deer will run, collapse, and run on, driven by terror for up to eight hours. Eventually, unable to force itself on, the hounds will catch up with it and may savage it unless there are hunt followers on hand to force the hounds back. The hunts say that a deer is always humanely killed with a single shot at the end of a day's sport, but it is almost impossible for an independent observer to witness the kill. The many kills that have accidentally been seen by residents or holiday visitors have mostly been violent and bloody affairs involving a shot or savaged deer crashing through gardens, swimming out to sea, being stabbed or having its throat slit by supporters.

Hindhunting

The cruelty of hindhunting is exacerbated by the fact that hinds are likely to be pregnant and/or have a dependent calf. They are also hunted at a time when they need to conserve their bodily resources to survive the winter months. Hind-hunting is basically operated in the same way as staghunting, except that tufters are not always used as any fit hind will do. The hunt is not after trophy heads. Because hinds lack the stamina of stags they may not run long enough to satisfy followers, so frequently more than one will be killed during a day's hunting. At the start of the season many hinds will have a dependent calf, born possibly as late as September. During the splitting up of the herd, calves unable to keep up or who cannot jump fences, get left behind. It is unlikely that these calves will ever be found again by their mothers. When a calf and hind are singled out for hunting the hind suffers anguish as her calf tires, often doubling back to try to urge it on. Eventually the hind is forced to abandon the calf, which is either killed by hounds or dies slowly of starvation, hypothermia or myopathy. When a hind can run no more she, like her calf, has no defence from the hounds and only if a huntsman is at hand will she avoid being savaged.

The kill

Once a deer has been killed members of the hunt eagerly seek trophies from the carcass. Feet and teeth are hacked from the body to be sold or given to supporters. A stag's's head is highly prized, but even the feet of an unborn calf are in great demand. Deer which managed to escape the hounds or who are inadvertently pursued during the day's hunt can also die. Hypothermia, brought on by loss of body

The cruelty of hindhunting is exacerbated by the fact that hinds are likely to be pregnant and/or have a dependent calf

heat (due to running through flooded rivers or driving rain) and myopathy (a fatal and agonising illness caused by stress), claim these uncounted victims.

Deer control

In the past, wild predators such as wolves would have selected the old, weak or lame deer, the object being a short chase and a quick kill. Conversely, the object of deer hunting with hounds is to provide a

long chase for the hunt followers. Exhausting the victim over a seven hour, twenty-five mile chase is clearly inefficient, expensive and obviously cruel. The West Country deer hunts kill approximately 150 deer a year, yet the Exmoor and Quantocks herds of 7-8,000 would require an annual cull in excess of 1,000 to maintain a stable population. Nationally each year at least 80,000 deer are killed by shooting. This is the method usually employed and accounts for 99% of the annual cull. Carefully controlled shooting will remove the old and sick deer and is necessary to maintain the correct sex ratio to avoid over-population. A skilled professional marksman using a high-powered rifle fitted with telescopic sights will kill a grazing deer instantly, humanely and efficiently.

The stag hunting controversy

**Some provocative questions . . . with straight answers.
From the Masters of Deerhounds Association**

Deer are such beautiful, gentle creatures; why should anyone be allowed them kill them?

Deer are large animals and very destructive to crops. Everyone, even those who wish to have staghunting banned, agrees that deer numbers must be controlled to prevent overpopulation which could lead to decimation by starvation and disease, and, indeed, to unacceptable damage to farming and forestry.

Could deer not control their own numbers naturally?

No. The red deer's only natural predator in Britain was the wolf, which has been extinct here for centuries; the necessary cull therefore must be carried out by man.

If deer have to be killed, surely that is no reason to make it into a sport?

The ethical basis of all field sports is the same, be it hunting, shooting, fishing, falconry or ferreting; in each case the quarry will be edible or a pest or, perhaps, both. As a result the animals involved will be killed whether their pursuit is a field sport or not. It is of no relevance to the hunted deer or the migrating salmon how their pursuers are motivated.

Yes, but why chase them? Why not shoot them so that they are killed instantly?

Shooting by rifle is in most parts of Britain the only practicable method of culling deer; it is effective for this

purpose. The problem with it is the irreducible risk of losing wounded deer; it is difficult enough killing deer in the wide open spaces of the Scottish Highlands where they are excluded from taking cover in woodland by deer-fencing; even there a small percentage – even with expert and experienced/professional stalkers – escapes wounded.

On staghunting ground in the 'West Country' (South West England) shooting deer is much more problematic. The small size of many landholdings (which makes the follow-up of a wounded deer illegal without permission), the extensive un-deerfenced woodland and the nocturnal nature of the species all make the loss of wounded animals more likely. Hunting makes deer temporarily tired, *but hunted deer never escape wounded.*

Furthermore deer are only killed instantly if shot in the head or neck – small targets and normally only taken at short range, and strongly disapproved of by the British Deer Society. Deer may run 50 yards; with a heart shot and 100 with a lung shot (the largest lethal and usual target); such deer are often close to woodland cover in the West Country and – following a misaimed first shot – the deer can quickly be in cover, deprive the rifle of a chance of a second shot, and possibly escape wounded.

In addition hunting ensures the survival of the fittest, which is not the case with shooting. Another point about shooting on Exmoor and the Quantocks is the danger to the general public which has unlimited access; hundreds of Americans are killed each year by deer 'hunters' in woodland not dissimilar to that where Staghunting takes place in the 'West Country'. It must also be borne in mind that currently up to five dozen injured deer are put out of their misery annually by the three 'West Country' packs; what would become of these unfortunates (some wounded – probably by poachers and some injured in accidents) many of whom would suffer a protracted and painful death if hunting were made illegal?

Are not staghunters using blackmail by stating, 'No hunting – no deer'?

No. They are stating what is obvious to country folk. It is the sporting interests which conserve the quarry species, be they salmon, grouse or deer. At present staghunting farmers provide an around-the-clock anti-poaching service and free access and passage for the deer to their valuable grazing and crops.

How can it be said that hunting is less cruel than shooting when some hunts last for 25 miles and eight hours?

A day's hunting consists of much more than the actual pursuit of a stag. Whilst the day may last for eight hours, although this would be unusual, the hunt itself would be much shorter. Time is needed to

Hunting ensures the survival of the fittest, which is not the case with shooting.

Photo: League Against Cruel Sports

locate the stag selected for culling by the harbourer, long periods may occur when the scent is lost or fresh deer intervene, and on some days when the harboured deer is completely lost, it may be necessary to start the process of finding a suitable cull animal from scratch half-way through the day.

Surely it is cruel to hunt a deer to a standstill?

Deer stand at bay as an active defence strategy evolved to counter their major natural predator, the wolf – not because they are run to exhaustion. Research has shown that large deer species do not rely solely on concealment and flight when attacked by wolves; they also engage in active defence, finding a suitable spot, often in water, where they can ward off attack with their antlers, or in the case of hinds with their sharp feet. This same instinctive strategy is used when hunted by hounds.

Even if shooting wounds some deer, how can you claim that hunting is more humane when hounds rip deer to pieces?

One of the commonest misconceptions is that deer are torn to pieces by the pack; this is not the case. At the end of a hunt the deer is either lost or stands at bay, in which case

hounds instinctively stand off and bay until the arrival of one of the hunt staff, with an approved firearm, who approaches the deer and shoots it at point blank range.

How can you justify hunting heavily pregnant hinds?

Heavily pregnant hinds are not hunted; hunting has to take place within seasons set – not by the hunts – but by Parliament. Fertile red deer hinds are normally either pregnant or accompanied by dependant calves. Parliament had to decide first whether hinds had to be killed at all; the answer to this was obvious. If control is necessary, and everyone agrees that it is then the breeding dynamics of the red deer makes killing hinds of critical importance to proper control. The next question was whether hinds should be killed when pregnant or when followed by dependant young. It would be cruel to kill milk hinds and leave calves to starve, so the season, set down by statute, is from 1 November to the end of February – a period when most healthy hinds will be pregnant, but not noticeably so, and calves at foot are self-sufficient.

• An extract from *'The Staghunting Controversy'*. See page 39 for details.

© Masters of Deerhounds Association December, 1994

Stag hunting – the facts

From The Royal Society for the Prevention of Cruelty to Animals (RSPCA)

The hunt is on

The red deer is Britain's largest wild animal and its numbers are regularly controlled in most parts of the country by trained marksmen. However, there are still people who use packs of hounds to hunt this majestic animal for sport.

There are three packs in the West Country – the Tiverton, Quantock, and Devon and Somerset – and another in the New Forest.

Hunting takes place between August and April, with different seasons for stags and hinds. The hunting seasons for red deer stags includes the period of the rut when stags are already under stress. The hunting season for hinds covers the time when most will be pregnant and will probably have last year's calf running with them.

Staghounds are bred for stamina rather than speed. The hunt of an individual deer will normally take several hours of continuous chase.

Under stress

Deer of all species are known to be highly susceptible to stress induced by outside influences. Victims of road accidents, though physically un-injured often die of shock. Myopathy, a usually fatal condition caused by stress, has been known in deer for many years and there is evidence that myopathy does arise following pursuit by staghounds. There can be no justification for continuing this cruelty. The RSPCA is totally opposed to the hunting of any animals with dogs. Stag hunting is a particularly cruel form of hunting which should be banned.

There is an alternative

Deer do not have many natural predators and the availability of vegetation means that the population would explode if it was not

> **Stag hunting is illegal in Scotland.**
>
> **There are four stag hunting packs in England.**
>
> **About 140 deer are hunted down each year.**

kept in check. They can cause significant damage to agriculture and forestry, so culling may be necessary. Most culls are undertaken by highly skilled marksmen who shoot selected animals with a rifle. If properly carried out, such shooting is comparatively humane. The three stag hunting packs in the West Country hunt and kill approximately ten fallow bucks each year, but 300-400 bucks and hinds still have to be shot.

The RSPCA's answer

It is grossly inhumane to pursue an animal for several hours to the point of exhaustion before it is killed.

Shooting by specialists is an efficient and comparatively humane method of population control, already widely practised, that can be used to control the deer population.

Some landowners believe stag-hunting acts as an incentive to deter poaching, but there is little justification for continuing one inhumane practice to control another. Legislation exists to control poaching and should be enforced.

Stag hunting makes an insignificant contribution to deer control in the West Country and the New Forest, and deer still have to be killed professionally.

Even if the deer succeeds in escaping the hunt, it may be left to die a lingering death from exhaustion and stress. Other animals in the herd may also panic and suffer the effects of stress.

RSPCA
December, 1994

Photo: League Against Cruel Sports

The RSPCA is totally opposed to the hunting of any animals with dogs.

INDEX

ADDITIONAL RESOURCES

You might like to contact the following organisations for further information. Due to the increasing cost of postage, many organisations cannot respond to inquiries unless they receive a stamped, addressed envelope.

Advocates for Animals
10 Queensferry Street
Edinburgh EH2 4PG
Tel: 0131 225 6039
Protects animals from cruelty and prevent the infliction of suffering. Produces a wide range of booklets on animal rights issues.

Animal Aid
7 Castle Street
Tonbridge
Kent TN9 1BH
Tel: 01732 364546
Opposed to any use of animals in medical research. Produces a wide range of booklets on animal rights issues.

Animals in Medical Research
12 Whitehall
London SW1A 2DY
Tel: 0171 588 0841
Supports the responsible use of animals in medical and biological research. Produces leaflets, videos, posters etc.

British Field Sports Society
59 Kennington Road
London SE1 7PZ
Tel: 0171 928 4742
Campaigns to ensure the continuation of field sports. They publish leaflets and student resources packs.

Biomedical Research Education Trust
58 Great Marlborough Street
London W1V 1DD
Tel: 0171 287 2818
Supports the responsible use of animals in medical research. Leaflets, factsheets, videos, speakers available.

British Union for the Abolition of Vivisection (BUAV)
16a Crane Close
London N7 8LB
Tel: 0171 700 4888
Strives for the total abolition of vivisection. Provides information to the public and the media.

Cosmetic Toiletry and Perfumery Association
Josaron House
5-7 John Princes Street
London W1M 9HD
Tel: 0171 491 8891
Fax: 0171 493 8061
Represents the cosmetics companies.

Dr. Hadwen Trust for Humane Research
22 Bancroft Street
Hitchin
Herts SG5 1JW
Tel: 01462 436819
Promotes the development of humane non-vivisectionist techniques of research without the use of living animals in order to replace animals experiments in science and medicine.

FRAME (Fund for the Replacement of Animals in Medical Experiments)
Russell & Burch House
96-98 North Sherwood Street
Nottingham NG4EE
Tel: 0115 958 4740
Works towards reducing the number animals used, refining methods to reduce suffering and replacing live animal methods with reliable alternative techniques.

Humane Research Trust (HRT)
Brook House
29 Bramhall Lane South
Bramhall
Cheshire SK7 2DN
Tel: 0161 439 8041
Fax: 061 439 3713
Supports medical and scientific research by advanced techniques which replace the use of laboratory animals.

Hunt Saboteurs
PO Box 1
Carlton
Nottingham NG4 3JY
Tel: 01602 590357
Campaigns for the protection of wildlife and to outlaw hunting.

League Against Cruel Sports (LACS)
83-87 Union Street
London SE1 1SG
Tel: 0171 403 6155
Campaigns for the protection of wildlife and to outlaw hunting with dogs. Leaflets and booklets available.

Master of Deerhounds Association
Abbots Park, Molland
South Molton
N. Devon
Campaigns to ensure the continuation of field sports. Leaflets and booklets available.

Research Defence Society (RDS)
58 Great Marlborough Street
London W1V 1DD
Tel: 0171 287 2818
Supports the responsible use of animals in medical and biological research. Leaflets, factsheets, videos and speakers available.

Research for Health Charities Group
PO Box 1417
Shepton Mallet
Somerset BA4 4YZ
Tel: 01749 890 771
Medical research charities in support of the responsible use of animals in medical research. Teacher and student discussion packs available.

RSPCA (Royal Society for the Prevention of Cruelty to Animals)
Causeway, Horsham
Sussex RH12 1HG
Tel: 01403 264181
Produces a wide range of leaflets and other materials on animal welfare issues. Contact the Enquiries Service.

Scottish Society for the Prevention of Cruelty to Animals (SSPCA)
19 Melville Street
Edinburgh EH3 7PL
Tel: 0131 224 6418
Produces leaflets and other materials on animal welfare issues.

ACKNOWLEDGEMENTS

The publisher is grateful for permission to reproduce the following material

Chapter One: Animal testing

Medical research and animal rights, © Research for Health Charities Group, December 1994, Opposing views about medical research and animal rights, © Research for Health Charities Group, September 1994, The moral issue, © Animal Aid, September 1994, Animals in scientific research – the statistics, © The Royal Society for the Prevention of Cruelty to Animals (RSPCA), September 1994, What medical advances have come from animal research?, © Biomedical Research Education Trust, September 1994, Animal experiments, © Animal Aid, September 1994, Medical research and drug testing, © Animal Aid, September 1994, Why is animal research necessary?, © Biomedical Medical Research Education Trust, September 1994, Some benefits of animal experimentation, © © Biomedical Medical Research Education Trust, September 1994, Why do we use animals for research?, © Humane Research Trust, September 1994, Animal experimentation, © Fund for the Replacement of Animals in Medical Experiments, November 1994, RSPCA policy on animal experimentation, © The Royal Society for the Prevention of Cruelty to Animals (RSPCA), September 1994, The hidden price of beauty, © Advocates for Animals, September 1994, Animal tests, © Animal Aid, September 1994, Animal experiments waste time, money and lives, © Dr Hadwen Trust, September 1994, Alternatives, © Research for Health Charities Group, December 1994, Alternatives, © Research for Health Charities Group, September 1994, Alternatives to animals in research, © Humane Research Trust, December 1994.

Chapter Two: Animal Sports

Worst hunt violence as hunting starts, © The Independent on Sunday, October 1994, The real animals, © The British Field Sports Society, September 1994, Video takes field sports campaign into schools, The Telegraph, London 1994, Thugs, wreckers and bullies, © The British Field Sports Society, November, 1994, The League Against Cruel Sports, © The League Against Cruel Sports, December 1994, Foxes and foxhunting, © The League Against Cruel Sports, September 1994, Fox hunting – Lets take action, © The Royal Society for the Prevention of Cruelty to Animals (RSPCA), September 1994, Hunting – the facts, , © The British Field Sports Society, November, 1994, Deer and staghunting, © The League Against Cruel Sports, September 1994, The staghunting controversy, Masters of Deerhounds Association, December 1994, Staghunting the facts, © The Royal Society for the Prevention of Cruelty to Animals (RSPCA), December 1994.

Photographs and illustrations

Page 1: Research for Health Charities Group, pages 6, 18, 21: Folio Collective, pages 7, 15, 16, 20: Animal Aid, pages 11, 17: Dr Hadwen Trust, page 13, Fund for the Replacement of Animals in Medical Research (FRAME), pages 22, 24, 33: British Field Sports Society, pages 23, 31: Ken Pyne, pages 26, 27, 28, 30, 34, 36, 37: League Against Cruel Sports.

Thanks

Martyn Lusher for typesetting.

Nick Parsons, from Data Direct, for research assistance.

Craig Donnellan
Cambridge
January, 1995